EMMA GOLDMAN
(1869–1940)
*Photograph reproduced by permission of
The Schlesinger Library, Radcliffe College.*

Emma Goldman

Twayne's United States Authors Series

David J. Nordloh, Editor

Indiana University, Bloomington

TUSAS 515

Emma Goldman

By Martha Solomon

Auburn University

Twayne Publishers
A Division of G.K. Hall & Co. • *Boston*

Emma Goldman

Martha Solomon

Copyediting supervised by Lewis DeSimone
Book production by Marne B. Sultz
Book design by Barbara Anderson

Typeset in 11 pt. Garamond
by Modern Graphics, Inc., Weymouth, Massachusetts

Printed on permanent/durable acid-free paper
and bound in the United States of America

Library of Congress Cataloging-in-Publication Data

Solomon, Martha.
  Emma Goldman.

  (Twayne's United States authors series ; TUSAS 515)
  Bibliography: p. 170
  Includes index.
  1. Goldman, Emma, 1869–1940. 2. Anarchists—United States—
Biography. 3. Communists—United States—Biography. I. Title. II. Series.
HX844.G6P44 1987   335′.83′0924 [B] 86–25677
ISBN 0-8057-7494-7

Contents

About the Author

Martha Solomon received her Ph.D. in psychology at the University of Texas at Austin. Currently she is a professor in the Department of Speech Communication at Auburn University in Auburn, Alabama. She has published essays in the *Quarterly Journal of Speech, Communication Education, Southern Speech Communication Journal, Communication Quarterly, Western Journal of Speech Communication,* and *Central States Speech Journal*. She is editor of the *Southern Speech Communication Journal* and is Vice President of the Southern Speech Communication Association.

Preface

Emma Goldman's life was so rich and so filled with public activity that reducing it to a single, brief volume is difficult. Her autobiography took almost a thousand pages to chronicle the details. Richard Drinnon's *Rebel in Paradise* condenses those details and enriches them with interpretation and historical background. Based on extensive and intensive research, his volume provides an excellent, careful summary of Goldman's life and includes an excellent bibliography. These two sources, the autobiography and Drinnon's work, contain most essential information about Goldman's public life. Two recent biographies by Candace Falk and Alice Wexler, which explore the personal and intimate dimensions of Goldman's life, provide a fuller picture of her as an individual and as a woman. This work will not attempt to compete with those, but will try, instead, to focus on Goldman as a writer and rhetorician. While I stand on their shoulders, I hope this work will extend the view by highlighting Goldman's writing and speaking as a propagandist for anarchism.

Chapter 1 gives a brief chronicle of Goldman's life with a focus on her development as an anarchist and on her activities as an agitator. Chapter 2 surveys the essays that explicate her general theories most fully, while chapter 3 treats her essays on contemporary social issues. Chapter 4 focuses on her work with literature, both as a publisher and as a dramatic critic. In doing so, it synthesizes her literary theory, examines her editorial practices, and discusses her critical methodology in *The Social Influence of the Modern Drama*. Chapter 5 treats her two historical works, *My Disillusionment in Russia* and *Living My Life*. Chapter 6 delineates the rhetorical dimensions of Goldman's writing and speaking and briefly describes her characteristic tone, organization, style, and delivery. Finally, chapter 7 assesses Goldman's significance and status as a rhetorician and anarchist.

The relationship between Goldman's essays and speeches deserves comment. In her autobiography she notes that most essays began as lectures, which she published in *Mother Earth* or separately as pamphlets. Comparisons of the length of her essays with reports of her speaking time suggest that she elaborated on and developed many points in her essays as she spoke, most probably with additional examples and responses to the audience's reactions. My examination of extant lecture notes reveals no substantial stylistic differences from the published essays except for misspellings. Very few lecture notes or texts are extant; on the other hand, Goldman suggested a close relationship between her essays and speeches. Thus, this discussion must focus primarily on her published articles, but with an emphasis on their similarity to her platform performances.

Martha Solomon

Auburn University

Acknowledgments

Scholarship is at the same time the most individual and the most communal of activities. Although each writer must struggle alone to develop a personal perspective on the materials that will enrich the perceptions of others, no researcher can work without the aid of earlier scholars, interested colleagues, helpful librarians, skillful secretaries, and a supportive, understanding family. This work has benefited greatly from these communal resources.

Grateful acknowledgment is made to Ian Ballantine for permission to quote from the Emma Goldman papers at the New York Public Library.

My colleagues deserve special thanks. Their interest together with their challenging questions and helpful suggestions sustained me and often renewed my enthusiasm. They heard more Emma Goldman stories than they bargained for, but they listened with good grace and even interest. The exchanges in our Common Room made my private efforts more productive.

The librarians at Ralph B. Draughon Library at Auburn were always helpful. Richard Shelton, who efficiently processed scores of interlibrary loan requests without complaint, was a valuable, if unpaid, assistant in this work. Mark McManus, whose thesis on Goldman profited from his skills as a librarian, shared his results with me. His knowledge and efforts expedited my research.

The secretaries, who typed from scarcely legible script, did meritorious service. Without Glenda Smith and Rita Dauber, there would have been no manuscript. They were a vital part of this scholarly effort.

To Wren, Trenna, and Cricket for their support on the home front I am especially grateful. They made many small sacrifices for the "book on Goldman." Finally, to Miller who was always willing to help in any way with any task, scholarly or familial, I owe major thanks. The book is dedicated to him, my scholarly colleague and personal companion.

These sources deserve credit for whatever merit the book possesses. Goldman, who lived this remarkable life, is the key to any interest it contains. The flaws are my own.

Chronology

1916 Sentenced to prison for dispensing birth control information.

1917 Sentenced to two years in prison for conspiring to avoid the draft; *Mother Earth* ceases publication.

1919 Deported to Russia with Berkman.

1921 Becomes disillusioned with Bolsheviks; leaves Russia.

1922 Writes seven articles for the *New York World* exposing the excesses of the Russia Revolution; publishes *My Disillusionment in Russia*.

1931 Publishes *Living My Life*.

1934 Returns to United States for a ninety-day lecture tour on drama because of special permission granted by U.S. government.

1936 Berkman commits suicide.

1936–1939 Works in England as a propagandist for the Spanish revolutionaries.

1940 Dies 14 May. Her body is returned to the United States for burial in Chicago.

Chapter One

An Anarchist's Biography

True Emancipation . . . begins in Woman's Soul.
——"The Tragedy of Woman's Emancipation"

"The next morning I woke as from a long illness. . . . I had a distinct sensation that something new and wonderful had been born in my soul . . . a great ideal, a burning faith, a determination to dedicate myself to the memory of my martyred comrades, to make their cause my own, to make known to the world their beautiful lives and heroic deaths."[1] Emma Goldman's strong emotional reaction to the execution of the Haymarket anarchists in November 1887 initiated her commitment to anarchism and marked the beginning of her lifelong political activism. Indeed, she called this event "the decisive influence in my life: that made me an Anarchist, a revolutionist."[2]

In writing her autobiography, *Living My Life,* Goldman focused on events, like the Haymarket executions, which marked her development as an anarchist activist, glossing over the broad historical context, her close personal relationships, and even her childhood. Indeed, she begins her autobiography with her arrival in New York City at age twenty, because she felt it was an emotional as well as a political turning point in her life. Despite her attention to her development as an anarchist, Goldman acknowledged that forces early in her life shaped the directions she would follow. The primary factor, she felt, was her innate personality. To one friend she wrote, "Environment can only bring out what is inherent in human beings. It can never put anything in sterile ground. If I had not been born with the love of freedom and the intense hatred of injustice, I do not believe that I would have become what I am."[3] Certainly, her accounts of her early childhood convey a surprisingly strong reaction to injustices of many sorts and a pronounced rebelliousness, which lend support to her theory. A more removed observer, however, can also perceive both historical events and personal experiences that at

1

least served to "bring out" her inherent qualities. In fact, Goldman's personal development and professional career are intimately tied to the historical milieu in which she lived.

Early Years in Europe: The Seeds of Rebellion

Born in Kovno (today Kaunas, Lithuania) on 27 June 1869, Emma Goldman by her accounts had a harsh and often humiliating child-hood. Her father, Abraham Goldman, apparently embittered and frustrated by repeated business failures, often vented his rages on the girl. Their precarious finances, stemming in part from her fa-ther's ineptitude and in part from racial prejudice against Jews, put further pressure on the family. Because she was a willful child, as she herself admitted, Emma suffered the beatings and humiliating discipline that her more docile siblings escaped. Despite her father's harshness, Emma wanted his affection; as she expressed it, "I wanted him to love me, but I never knew how to reach his heart. His harshness served only to make me more contrary" (11–13, 59–60).

Aside from the tensions within the family, which evoked Emma's natural recalcitrance, she later identified other small incidents as influential. Her father's defeat in a local election allegedly because of his Jewishness and his failure to provide adequate vodka for the "debased and brutalized mob" made her wary of "putting any trust in politics." The brutality of military officers toward the soldiers and the dismissal of an unmarried pregnant nursemaid, whom she dearly loved, were other episodes that she recalled as rousing and heightening her moral sensibility.[4]

When the family moved to Königsberg (the capital of Prussia and a major Baltic seaport), Emma attended school briefly, her only formal education; but it was also a painful and disappointing ex-perience. Her religion instructor beat the palms of recalcitrant stu-dents with a ruler, while her geography teacher sexually harassed the girls. Only her German instructor encouraged Emma to remain in Königsberg when her family moved to St. Petersburg in 1881, offering to tutor her for the gymnasium. Her religion teacher refused to give her the requisite certificate of good character, however, saying that she "had none" and "was a terrible child and would grow into a worse woman." Prophetically, he noted that she "had no respect for . . . her elders or for authority"(118).

She said that her year in St. Petersburg, despite her initial reluctance to move, "changed my very being and the whole course of my life."[5] As Alice Wexler notes, Goldman "had arrived in the Russian capital at a critical historical moment." Czar Alexander II, whose early reign had promised better conditions for the peasants and the Jews, had been assassinated by a terrorist group associated with a Russian socialist movement.[6] Although Goldman's mother had castigated the assassins because of her conviction that the czar had helped the Jews, Goldman soon developed a sympathy for them. The repression of dissent and the mistreatment of many innocent groups, which followed the assassination, intensified her identification with the "Nihilists," as she labeled them. In the clandestine reading and discussion groups that sprang up in response to the repressive policies, Goldman's "spirit caught the white flame of Russian idealism. . . . I was too young to understand and grasp the theories that carried Russian youth forward. But my soul became imbued with the humanitarian ideas everywhere in the air. Added to this was the hatred and the persecution of the Jews, which I could not help but see, and which stirred me profoundly."[7] The people punished for the assassination became her "heroes and martyrs, henceforth my guiding stars" (28).

One particularly significant aspect of Goldman's brief political education in St. Petersburg was her growing awareness of the role women could play in revolutionary activities. The heroines of books she read during this period impressed her, particularly Vera Pavlovna in Chernyshevsky's *What Is to Be Done?* Tales of real Russian heroines like Vera Zassulich were even more inspiring. Indeed, Goldman hoped to emulate these women and do her part for the revolution. This early consciousness of women as equal partners with men in the struggle for social change helped shape Goldman's later commitment to feminist causes (26–29).

Bored by the tedious work in a St. Petersburg factory, castigated by her father as a loose woman because of her sexual adventures, and eager for the freedom she envisioned in America, Goldman intensely wanted to join her stepsister Helena in emigrating to join their sister Lena, who was married and already living in Rochester, New York. With her father's reluctant agreement, the two sisters left for America in December of 1885 (11).

Like most immigrants, sixteen-year-old Emma had bright hopes for America. "The last day of our journey comes vividly to mind. . . . Helena and I stood pressed to each other, enraptured by the sight of harbour and the Statue of Liberty suddenly emerging from the mist. Ah, there she was, the symbol of hope, of freedom, of opportunity! . . . We, too, Helena and I, would find a place in the generous heart of America. Our spirits were high, our eyes filled with tears" (11).

Unfortunately, like many other immigrants, her hopes were disappointed by the realities of working-class life. Not only was stolid Rochester itself a boring contrast to the exciting Königsberg and St. Petersburg, but Goldman's personal life was also constraining. The rapid pace, rigid discipline, and insensitive bosses in the "model factory" in which she first worked quickly disillusioned her about capitalism, nourishing her lifelong antipathy toward it. A second job in a less pressured factory brought her into contact with Jacob Kersner, a well-educated immigrant from Odessa, in the Ukrainian Republic, who offered her companionship and, she first thought, shared her interest in books.[8] Despite her reluctance and Helena's antagonism toward him, Kersner's insistence compelled her into an engagement. Her mother and father's arrival in Rochester strained Emma and Helena's resources, causing them to accept Kersner as a boarder in their small house. With the reunion of the family, a situation from which she had sought to escape in Russia, Goldman found life "unbearable." Only her interest in the Haymarket events, which were covered in lurid detail in the press, saved her from "utter despair" during this period (18–25). Because Goldman saw Haymarket as crucial in her development, some knowledge of these events is vital for an understanding of her career.

The Haymarket Affair: Early Anarchist Sympathies

The Haymarket affair, which Goldman followed closely in the press, was, in Paul Avrich's words, "a pivotal event in the history of both the anarchist and labor movements."[9] As Henry David notes, "the Haymarket affair is of major significance in the annals of American labor and jurisprudence, while the background which made it possible and gives it meaning constitute an important chapter of the social-revolutionary movement in the United States."[10] Although the bomb-throwing, which killed and wounded several policemen on 4 May 1886, was the culmination of a particular sequence of events associated with a strike at the McCormick Reaper Works in Chicago, the roots of the Haymarket incident go much deeper.

The 1880s were an exceptionally tumultuous period for the labor movement in the United States. As the pace of industrial development quickened, more workers joined labor organizations in an attempt to gain both greater benefits and some protections. Indeed, conditions for workers were often grim: low wages forced many to endure poverty; living conditions were sometimes shocking; and employment was irregular. Unfortunately, many employers were insensitive to or even denied the plight of their workers.[11] Goldman's first experience with employers' attitudes in Rochester demonstrates the abuse which workers confronted. Her request for a modest raise was met with scorn and deprecating remarks about her "extravagant tastes," because she mentioned that her wages were inadequate not only to cover her small expenses but also to permit her to buy an occasional ticket to the theater. Her employer was, of course, surrounded by luxury, including an entire vase of roses, of which Goldman could not even afford a single blossom on her salary (17). The labor leader Samuel Gompers quotes one manufacturer as saying, "I regard my employees as I do a machine, to be used to my advantage, and when they are old and of no further use I cast them in the street."[12] Denied protection under law, workers increasingly turned to unions and strikes to assert their demands.

Although all large urban areas had active labor groups, Chicago and New York became the centers for the more radical groups, especially for the socialists and anarchists.[13] Chicago's large foreign population was one factor accounting for the prominence of such groups there, because European immigrants had proved much more receptive to radical doctrines than native-born workers. According to Avrich, in 1878 the Socialist Labor party (SLP) in Chicago "boasted nearly a thousand activists, issued newspapers in three languages, and enjoyed the support of a growing number of working men."[14] In 1883 the location there of the Information Bureau for the Socialist Federation of America suggests the extent of anarchist and communist activity in the city.[15]

Despite its growth, however, the radical facet of the labor movement lacked focus and cohesion until 1882. The arrival of Johann Most in New York and his extensive national lecture tour galvanized the movement. Most, who later became Goldman's mentor, was already a well-known anarchist agitator in Europe. He was editor of *Die Freiheit* and "one of the greatest revolutionary orators of his time." His Chicago speech in December 1882 denouncing capitalists and others who oppressed labor attracted an overflow crowd of six thousand and produced wild applause.[16] Not only did Most vehemently attack "money kings, railroad magnates, coal barons, and factory lords," but he urged violent action against them.[17] In 1885 Most published a pamphlet, *Science of Revolutionary Warfare*, which provided instructions for the manufacture and use of bombs and other terrorist devices.[18] His forceful, concrete advocacy of violence was a key factor in establishing the aggressive attitude of the radical labor group in Chicago. An economic depression between 1883–86 further encouraged the growth of the International Working People's Association (IWPA), a revolutionary labor group composed primarily of immigrants.

When more moderate organizations like the Federation of Organized Trade and Labor Unions (the forerunner of the American Federation of Labor) proposed strikes on 1 May 1886 to enforce the eight-hour-day system, the IWPA joined in although the leaders saw such actions as largely futile and temporizing.[19] In Chicago the peaceful demonstrations on 1 May, which drew large crowds, were bitterly denounced by business leaders and the press. Then, on 3 May at the McCormick Reaper Works, violence erupted between strikers and scabs, which left two workers dead. Although the IWPA and the anarchists were not involved in this incident, they soon issued leaflets urging "revenge" and calling workers to arm to "destroy the hideous monster that seeks to destroy you."[20] At a meeting on 4 May to protest police brutality in the incident, prominent Chicago anarchists spoke on behalf of the workers and the eight-hour day, but apparently did not advocate violent reprisals. As police began to disperse the crowd, a still unidentified person hurled a bomb into their midst, killing seven of them as well as an unknown number of onlookers.[21]

Public reaction was immediate and virtually unanimous in its condemnation not only of the incident but especially of the anarchists associated with it. The *Chicago Tribune* called the anarchists "vipers," "ungrateful hyenas," and "serpents." The *New York Times* called them "cut-throats" and urged "the promptest and sternest way of dealing" with the "anarchist murder of policemen in Chicago." Other newspapers focused on the anarchists as immigrants, labeled them "foreign savages," and urged their deportation.[22] As Avrich notes, "News of the incident provoked a nationwide convulsion of deep-rooted and violent prejudice. . . . A fear of subversion seized the country, triggering a campaign of radical-baiting rarely if ever surpassed."[23]

Prominent Chicago anarchists, including Albert Parsons and August Spies, editors of *The Alarm,* were quickly indicted for the crime, although there was no evidence to connect them with the bomb itself. The ensuing trial "took place in an atmosphere of unparalleled prejudice," with both press and public demanding their conviction and execution.[24] Although the trial lasted from 21 June until 20 August, the outcome was clear much earlier. Both public and press enthusiastically endorsed the guilty verdict and the sentence of execution.[25]

Goldman's interest in and sympathy for the Chicago anarchists were predictable. A worker herself, she was keenly aware of the abuses of the capitalist system. Moreover, her empathy for the Russian revolutionaries drew her toward the radical policies of groups like those in Chicago. When she and Helena began attending socialist meetings in Rochester, she also heard Johanna Greie, a well-known German socialist speaker, defend the Haymarket anarchists in an emotionally moving talk. Soon she began reading *Die Freiheit,* Johann Most's paper, which "breathed deep hatred of the powers that were preparing the crime in Chicago." What she read in Most's paper excited her interest in the men involved in anarchism. "I began to read *Die Freiheit* regularly. I sent for the literature advertised in the paper and I devoured every line on anarchism I could get. . . . I saw a new world opening before me" (9–10). The more she heard, the more emotionally involved she became with a radical movement that she only dimly understood at first. Many years later, Goldman recalled the impact of the event:

Like many other immigrants of forty years ago, I came to the United States with an exalted idea of American liberties, and with sincere belief in this country as a haven for the oppressed, with her wonderful equality of opportunity. That was in 1886. Then came my own first experiences with the crushing industrial machine. I worked ten hours a day in a factory, in Rochester, New York for the munificent sum of two dollars and fifty cents a week, and there I gradually learned to see things in a different light. The great strike in Illinois which led up to the Haymarket riots, the bomb explosion, the arrest of the Chicago anarchists, their farcical

trial and terrible end—these were my early lessons in American liberty.
I was perfectly innocent of social ideals at the time, but my native rebelliousness against injustice and wrong, and my innate consciousness of
what was real and false in the press of the country, gave me the first
impulse towards the vision for which the Chicago men had been done to
death by the blind furies of wealth and power.[26]

The Budding Anarchist

During the period of her keen interest in the Haymarket events,
other elements of Goldman's personal life were unpleasant and frustrating. Pressures from Kersner to marry him and the close contact
with her parents in the small house left her tense and miserable.
Her desire to escape again and her unhappiness forced her reluctantly
into an abortive marriage in February 1887. Boredom, financial
problems, and sexual frustration (Kersner was impotent) soon undermined the marriage. After ten months, Goldman sought a divorce
and moved to New Haven, where she mingled excitedly with young
socialists and anarchists. Although her life in New Haven was more
stimulating, physical problems forced her to return to Rochester to
live with Helena, now married and with a child (18–25). Urged
by both Kersner and her family, she remarried him, but their
incompatibilities were still too great. To escape the ostracism of the
community because of her second divorce and to learn more about
socialism and anarchism, which she had begun to explore in Rochester and New Haven, Goldman moved to New York, a center of
radical activity, in 1889.

She later insisted that this was the most significant moment of
her life: "It was the starting point that made me aware of all that
preceded the 15th of August 1889 and all that happened after."[27]
Newly drawn to the anarchist movement, Goldman immediately
gravitated to the lower East Side, the hub of their activity. There
she met two men who influenced her transformation into the primary
spokesperson for American anarchism: Johann Most and Alexander
Berkman.

As editor of *Die Freiheit,* Johann Most had already stirred Goldman
with his powerful prose. The newspaper accounts of him in relation
to the Haymarket tragedy had heightened her interest. "During
this entire time the newspapers of Rochester were filled with hair-
raising stories about Johann Most and his evil deeds. They aroused
my interest, but in quite a different way from that intended. I

determined to know the man."[28] His dynamic delivery and eloquence as he spoke against those involved in the execution of the Haymarket anarchists overwhelmed Emma, shaking her to her very roots. His immediate personal interest in her and his generous offer of books intensified her earlier enthusiasm. She became an avid disciple (6, 29–36).

When Goldman met Most in 1889, he was forty-three and, after only a few years in America, the most prominent anarchist orator in the country.[29] He derived his reputation largely from his long and well-known history of radical activities in Europe. Born in Augsburg, Germany, in 1846, Most was the illegitimate child of an office clerk and a governess. At seventeen he left home and began traveling around central Europe working as a bookbinder and learning about politics. He was soon drawn into radical circles and became an effective orator despite a facial disfigurement that had haunted him in early childhood. When he was imprisoned in Austria in 1869 merely for speaking to a group of workers on strike to protest a government action, the government's unfair actions toward him enhanced his reputation as an agitator and increased his influence with workers.

After another brief imprisonment for political agitation, Most was elected to the German Reichstag. Bismarck, however, arousing fears against radicals like Most, convinced the body to dissolve itself. Most was soon in prison again on slight charges. London seemed a more promising center for his radical agitation; therefore, Most moved there and began publishing *Die Freiheit,* a socialist newspaper in German. Soon he was the hero of German socialists everywhere.

Because of his differences with Karl Marx, however, Most was soon expelled from the Social Democratic party. In contrast to Marx, Most opposed a centralized state to control affairs after the abolition of capitalism. Indeed, he felt that any centralized state because of its coercive capabilities actually oppressed workers more than a capitalistic economic system. He also favored education as a means to achieve anarchist ends rather than violent overthrow of capitalism. Because of their differences, Marx deliberately undermined Most's position in the Social Democratic party. In turn, the Social Democrats denounced Most for having "committed actions which were opposed to all laws of honesty." Then Most's editorial support in *Die Freiheit* for the terrorist assassination of Czar Alexander II further eroded his popularity in England.

The invitation from the Social Revolutionary Club of New York to lecture throughout the United States gave him another, more promising arena. His tour in 1882–83 immediately made him the leader of the German-speaking social revolutionary movement in the United States and helped to unify other radical groups around his banner. His resumed publication of *Die Freiheit* in New York City sustained his influence among German immigrants in America and abroad. As mentioned earlier, his advocacy of violence in Chicago probably helped shape the attitudes that produced the Haymarket riot.

During his years in the United States until his death in 1906, Most continued both his fiery writing and speaking for anarchism. His advocating of acts of violence when they were legitimate responses to oppression and his sustained political agitation attracted continual police attention and harassment. In fact, he was arrested and convicted in 1886 after the Haymarket incident simply on the basis of his earlier published pamphlet, the *Science of Revolutionary Warfare*. After the assassination of President McKinley in 1901, Most was again imprisoned, this time for reprinting a fifty-year-old essay on violence in *Die Freiheit* the day before the assassination.

Meeting Most in 1889, when he was at the height of his prominence, was significant for Goldman in several ways. His support for the assassins of Alexander II, Goldman's girlhood idols, and of the Haymarket anarchists undoubtedly gave him great credibility for her. Thus, she was drawn toward his anarchist views and away from the socialist theories that had also intrigued her. Moreover, his effectiveness and prominence as both an orator and a writer provided a model for her later activities. An equally significant element was his interest in art and literature, which he communicated to her. Long after Most's death, she admitted, "We owed much to Most, I more than the others. It was he who had been my teacher, my guide into a new world of social ideas, to new beauty in art and music. Most loved both intensely and helped me to learn to love them."[30]

Most, on his part, saw Goldman's potential. When she related her childhood experiences, he astutely perceived her natural talent as a speaker and vowed to make her a great orator and his successor as a propagandist. At his insistence, despite her initial nervousness and sense of inadequacy, Goldman began speaking in public. Within a few months, by February 1890, she went on her first tour, lecturing in Yiddish (40,47).

Her experiences on this initial tour, though sometimes frustrating and embarrassing, were important to her development as a propagandist orator. In her first presentation in Buffalo she spoke inspiringly, but later realized she had not adequately addressed her topic and, consequently, had done little good for the anarchist cause. Of her performance in Cleveland she wrote: "It was not a meeting, it was a circus, and I was the clown" (52). She was particularly chagrined by the questions of an elderly worker who pointed out the weaknesses in the arguments Most had provided for her. "My first public experience did not bring the result Most had hoped for," she said, "but it taught me a valuable lesson. It cured me somewhat of my childlike faith in the infallibility of my teacher and impressed on me the need of independent thinking" (52–53). The experience also brought another, happier realization: "I could sway people with words. . . . I wept with the joy of knowing" (51).

If the tour opened Goldman's eyes to her mentor's limitations, her gradual realization of his attitude toward her as a woman further disillusioned her. Goldman wanted to be an independent comrade; Most wanted a submissive disciple and mistress. Gradually, their intimacy evaporated and Goldman was drawn more closely to Alexander Berkman (53, 72–73). Like Goldman Berkman was a Russian Jew, but his childhood had been far less traumatic. Born in Lithuania in 1870, he enjoyed all the comforts and privileges his well-off parents could provide.[31] Nevertheless, like Goldman, he was naturally sensitive to human suffering and intolerant of the abuses of class and power that he observed during his childhood in St. Petersburg. Moreover, Berkman's favorite uncle, Maxim Natanson, who fled abruptly after the assassination of the czar in 1881, was deeply involved in the revolutionary movement and undoubtedly influenced the young boy, despite Berkman's parents' condemnation of the Nihilists responsible for the deed.[32] After his father's death and perhaps in reaction to the control of a more conservative uncle over his life, Berkman began to associate with radical students from the university in St. Petersburg and, like Goldman, became imbued with a revolutionary fervor he only dimly understood.

When his mother died and he no longer had roots in Russia, Berkman, age eighteen, drifted first to Germany and then to the United States. Settling on the lower East Side of New York City, he worked alternately as a cigar maker, cloak maker, and printer, despite his education in a gymnasium. Living the life of a worker in New York City, he became deeply committed to anarchism and hoped to be the ideal revolutionist who would gladly sacrifice himself "on the altar of the beloved People."[33] Indeed, Berkman's willingness, even eagerness, to die for the cause was to play an important role in his and Goldman's plan to assassinate Henry Clay Frick in the wake of the Homestead strike.

Although as a revolutionist he eschewed personal involvements, Berkman found both comrade and lover in Goldman. His enormous energy first attracted her, but their shared values and similar backgrounds nourished the relationship. Of the many men in her later life only Berkman, she believed, had respected her independence sufficiently not to pressure her to fill the traditional role of wife and mother. Berkman's steadfastness and dedication to anarchism helped to make him the central figure in her emotional life, even during his long imprisonment for the attack on Henry Clay Frick. As Wexler notes, "Emma always looked up to the more educated Berkman, constantly compared herself to him, respected his views even when she did not agree with them, and cared desperately about his opinion of her."[34]

In these early months in New York, Goldman's developing relationships with Most and Berkman and her increasing political involvement through work at the *Freiheit* office and in anarchist meetings dramatically altered her perspective. Coming back to New York City, she had hoped to learn more about both anarchism and socialism. Within six months, Goldman had lost her interest in socialism, was deeply involved with the leaders of the anarchist movement, and was dedicating herself fully to it. Because she was uncertain of her English and lectured primarily in Yiddish or German, her efforts were directed almost exclusively toward fellow immigrants, who were strongly drawn toward radical politics. The Homestead strike of May 1892, another crucial event in her life, led indirectly to her becoming an advocate to native American workers.

Homestead, Frick, and Blackwell's Island

When Goldman and Berkman learned of the Homestead strike and its repercussions, they were running an ice-cream parlor and lunchroom in Worcester, Massachusetts, to earn funds to return to Russia and work for the revolution there. The clash between the increasingly powerful Amalgamated Association of Iron and Steel Workers of America and the Carnegie-owned steel mills in Homestead, Pennsylvania, managed by Henry Clay Frick, abruptly changed their plans. Having already supported workers in strikes in New York City, both saw the dramatic events at Homestead as an opportunity to further the anarchist cause. Because of his role in the incident, Frick became the focus of their activities.

At forty-two, a millionaire and a partner with Andrew Carnegie in the company, Frick had a reputation as a hard-nosed businessman and an opponent of unions. Still, he had been willing to negotiate with union leaders despite pressure in letters from chief owner Andrew Carnegie, vacationing in Scotland, who wished to operate the mill as a nonunion plant. Frick had also gotten assurance from the Pinkerton agency that it could supply enough men to protect the plant if a strike occurred. After a meeting on 23 June ended in a stalemate, Frick took action. Although the union contract had another week to run, he terminated negotiations and announced that the company would in the future bargain individually rather than collectively with workers.[35] Although the wages and the termination date of the new contract had been chief issues in the negotiations, union recognition and collective bargaining were the new focus. At Frick's direction, the mill's management locked out eight hundred workers on 28 June and by 29 June all the strikers had been formally discharged. The union quickly organized a twenty-four-hour watch around the plant to prevent strikebreakers from entering.

Early on the morning of 6 July, Pinkerton agents arrived by barges to surround the plant in this tense situation. At first thinking the barges carried strikebreakers, the boycotting strikers rushed to prevent their landing. The ensuing battle left seven Pinkerton agents and nine strikers dead and many others wounded. The National Guard was summoned to restore order.

In contrast to the unsympathetic reaction to the strikers at Haymarket six years earlier, the press immediately condemned the use of the Pinkertons and castigated Frick. The *Chicago Herald* compared Frick to Simon Legree, while the *New York World* called his ban on unionism "the attempt of an arbitrary and tyrannical man to impose his will upon men as free as himself."[36] On 7 July Congress passed a resolution providing for an investigation of the events, and later that summer the Senate authorized an inquiry into the use of private armed guards.

In the context of this heightened awareness of workers' problems and sympathy for labor groups, Berkman, long committed to sacrificing himself for the cause, felt the time was right for an *attentat:* an act of political violence that would dramatize their revolutionary cause and galvanize workers to overthrow capitalism. Assassinating Frick, who had already been publicly condemned by the press, he believed, would stimulate public support for anarchism. Although Berkman insisted on acting alone to avoid the unnecessary sacrifice of other lives, Goldman was to raise money for a revolver and for a new suit to aid Berkman in gaining admittance to Frick's office. When a fellow anarchist who had a small fund for propaganda activities refused support and when Goldman's amateurish attempt at prostitution was a miserable failure, she got the money from Helena on the pretext of illness (90–95).

In his assassination attempt on 23 July, Berkman only managed to wound Frick and was quickly apprehended. With Berkman in jail for a crime she had helped plan, Goldman composed her first serious journalistic piece for the *Anarchist,* "Alexander Berkman, the avenger of the murdered Homestead men" (98). In the days that followed, she worked diligently to garner public support for him. When Most criticized her support of political assassination, Goldman challenged him and on one occasion even horsewhipped him publicly (105–6). Despite her actions, however, public opinion rose against Berkman. Ironically, even the union committee that was coordinating the Haymarket strike condemned his act as "unlawful" and expressed its "sympathy" with Frick.[37]

In a hasty trial hindered by an inept translator, Berkman pleaded his own case in Russian. Partially because of his legal inexperience, he failed to protest the actions of the court during the proceedings, an oversight that thwarted his later attempts at legal appeal. Without leaving their seats, the jury found him guilty of felonious assault, and the judge sentenced him to three seven-year terms to run consecutively, plus one year for carrying a concealed weapon, a total of twenty-two years in prison. Both Berkman and Goldman were stunned with the harshness of the sentence: they had expected a single seven-year term. The harshness of the sentence and the injustice of Berkman's trial fuelled Goldman's enthusiasm for anarchism, by reinforcing her ideas about the state's abuses of personal liberty (106–7).

When Berkman began serving his sentence, Goldman's first months alone were difficult and depressing. Not only was she plagued by ill health, but her connection with Berkman and her public support of him also made it difficult for her to find a room: she ended up in a brothel, the only place willing to rent to her. Although neither she nor Berkman acknowledged her role in the attack on Frick, police harassed her in an attempt to link her to the crime. At one of her lectures during this bleak period, she luckily met Edward Brady, who had just been released from an Austrian prison for his anarchist activities. Lonely and unhappy, Goldman was strongly attracted to him. Brady's expression of admiration and sympathy for Berkman's attempt impressed her still more. His kindness and concern developed into love and the two were soon deeply involved. Brady, whom Goldman called "the most scholarly man I ever met," proved to be another valuable mentor (113). Under his tutelage, Goldman read the writings of Shakespeare, Goethe, Rousseau, and Voltaire. He also introduced her to the saloon of Justus Schwab, the most famous radical center in New York. At the Schwab saloon, Goldman mixed and argued with the radical artists and literati of the city. On an intimate level, Goldman found sexual happiness and personal security with Brady, who encouraged her in her activities. Although Brady's desire for a child eventually undermined the relationship, his support was crucial to Goldman during the initial period of her separation from Berkman (115–21).

But Goldman's domestic happiness was soon disrupted by her political activities. Asked to speak at a rally of the unemployed in Union Square during the depression of 1893, Goldman abandoned her careful notes when she saw the throngs waiting to hear her. After a spirited attack on the wealthy, according to her own account, she concluded: "Demonstrate before the palaces of the rich; demand work. If they do not give you work, demand bread. If they deny you both, take bread. It is your sacred right" (123). These impromptu remarks, together with earlier ones in a similar vein, led to her arrest on 30 August on charges of inciting to riot. This experience made her leery in later years of departing too far from her prepared text. Despite what she termed a brilliant address by her lawyer and despite the obvious flaws in the prosecution's case (no concrete records of her statements existed), the jury found her guilty. On 18 October the judge sentenced her to one year in Blackwell's Island Penitentiary (129–30).

Surprisingly the months in prison were beneficial. The prison physician recruited her as his assistant; her natural aptitude and her compassion for the prisoners made Goldman a fine nurse. She found the work rewarding. Moreover, prison provided leisure to read free from the pressures from her fellow anarchists. Besides learning a new vocation, she also gained intellectual confidence and resolve. "Here . . . I learned to see life through my own eyes not those of Sasha, Most, or Ed. . . . The prison had been the crucible that tested my faith. It had helped me to discover strength in my own being, the strength to stand alone, the strength to live my life and fight for my ideals against the whole world if need be. The State of New York could have rendered me no greater service than by sending me to Blackwell's Island Penitentiary" (136–37, 148).

These months yielded another significant result. In working with the prisoners, Goldman became increasingly fluent in English. Through the kindness of John Swinton, a prominent New York journalist sympathetic to radical causes, she also recognized the political idealism of some successful, native Americans and saw a new audience to which she could direct her efforts. These two factors convinced her to devote herself to propaganda in English, among American people, for she was now convinced that "real social changes could be accomplished only by the natives" (155).

Nurse and Lecturer: 1895–1901

After her release from the penitentiary in 1894, Goldman worked in tenements and slums as a practical nurse and midwife. Nursing made her financially self-sufficient and gave her enough free time to devote to her anarchist activities. She needed further training to become a licensed nurse, however. Promised support by Berkman's cousin Modest Stein—an old friend who had become a successful commercial artist—and lured by the excitement of Vienna, Goldman sailed for Europe on 15 August 1895 to study at the Allgemeines Krankenhaus in Vienna, exactly six years after her arrival in New York (162). En route in England, she caused "quite a sensation" with her lectures on anarchism.[38] She even engaged in the traditional practice of speaking in Hyde Park. Although the hecklers bewildered her initially because she was unused to such interruptions, Goldman quickly regained her poise and became an effective stump speaker (163–68). Moreover, in London she met three prominent anarchists: Peter Kropotkin, whom she had long admired; Errico Malatesta, a well-known Italian; and Louise Michel, a militant leader in the French Commune. The beginning of the term in Vienna forced her to leave England, a place in which she had experienced "glorious days enriched by personal contact with her great leaders" (169).

Her year in Vienna proved equally fruitful. Her studies at the hospital under the name "Mrs. E. G. Brady" included a series of lectures by Sigmund Freud, whose talks "helped me to understand myself, my own needs" (173). Equally important, Freud's theories alerted her to the effects of sexual repression on human beings, a theme she would later treat extensively in her talks. Other professors, though their topics were less personally relevant, broadened her medical knowledge. At the same time she attended public lectures on modern German prose and poetry. Goldman was particularly drawn to the works of Nietzsche, which she read voraciously. She attended plays and operas, thrilling to Wagner's music and especially moved by a performance by Eleonora Duse, a much admired actress of the day, as Magda in Sudermann's *Heimat*. When Stein sent Goldman return fare and an extra hundred dollars to buy new clothes, she preferred to invest her money in "my beloved books, purchasing a supply of the works of the writers that were making literary history, especially the dramatists. No amount of wardrobe could have given me so much joy as my precious little library," she later recalled (172–74). This brief, intense exposure to European culture and thought impressed Goldman deeply. Increasingly she perceived in European literature, particularly in the works of Hauptman, Ibsen, and Strindberg, an artistic depiction of anarchist themes. Nietzsche became a model of the creative spirit, the quintessential anarchist (194).

When she returned to the United States, Goldman resumed her nursing. As a midwife, she was often called to tenements where she observed firsthand the plight of women who were bearing unwanted children for whom they could not adequately care. The drastic measures these women resorted to in attempts to produce abortions depressed her, especially because she did not feel competent to provide that service herself and also because she could offer no

practical advice on how to avoid becoming pregnant. These experiences sensitized her to the burden that childbearing imposed on
poor women and to the need for contraceptive information. These
problems were, she felt, more pressing even than the need for social
revolution (186).

During the period between her return in 1896 to the assassination
of McKinley in 1901, Goldman increased her circle of friends and
her public visibility. She lectured coast to coast: in Philadelphia,
Detroit, Pittsburgh, Cleveland, Cincinnati, Chicago, St. Louis,
Denver, San Francisco, Los Angeles, and San Jose. True to her goal
of reaching the natives, she spoke in English, but she did little else
to mollify her American audiences. She developed a frank, flamboyant style that intensified her notoriety and probably increased
her audiences. For example, when Goldman was invited by a Con-
gregationalist minister in Detroit to discuss anarchism, she avoided
controversy in her prepared speech, but questions from the audience
elicited candid and inflammatory answers: "I came here to avoid as
much as possible treading on your corns. . . . I see now that it
was a mistake. If one enters battle, he cannot be squeamish about
a few corns." Her further answers brought cries of "Blasphemy!
Heretic! Sinner! . . . Throw her out!" Finally, her retort to a hostile
question about free love produced pandemonium. Even Robert In-
gersoll, the famous agnostic, condemned her performance. The minister was forced to resign, but Goldman continued her tour, more
famous than ever (206–7).

As her notoriety grew, Goldman's invitations to speak to labor
organizations and worker groups increased, her audiences broadened,
and she gained confidence. Her flamboyance as a speaker undoubtedly attracted many curious spectators to see the infamous "Red
Emma," as she was later called. Optimistically perceiving a recep-
tivity through the country for radical ideas and radical theories, she
was eager to extend her activities.[39] She was well on her way to
becoming the premier spokesperson for anarchism that Most had
envisioned (213–26). Since her lectures generated little revenue,
she was faced with earning a living. Goldman's success as a nurse
and her interest in medicine drew her toward becoming a physician.
When two sympathetic Detroit businessmen offered to support further medical studies in Europe, Goldman readily accepted their
offer. It had the additional lure of allowing her to attend an anarchist

conference planned for Paris. She sailed again for London in the fall of 1899 with plans to lecture there en route to Paris (246, 250).

Arriving in London on 13 November 1899 at the height of public arousal over the Boer War, Goldman made antiwar lectures despite warnings from her friends. When one booing crowd seemed hopelessly hostile, Goldman appealed to their English traditions of justice and liberty, referring to the works of Shakespeare, Milton, Byron, Shelley, and Keats as examples of the view she represented. The audience was bewildered into silence by her approach. Goldman reported later: "I delivered my lecture on war and patriotism as I had given it all through the United States, merely changing the parts that had dealt with the causes of the Spanish-American hostilities to those behind the Anglo-Boer War. . . . The house went wild" (256). Clearly, Goldman was coming to relish lively exchanges with her audiences and to enjoy her rhetorical hold over them.

Once in Paris, Goldman became more deeply involved with her new lover. Invigorated by the cultural riches of the city and the anarchist activities there, Goldman lost interest in continuing her medical studies. A letter from one sponsor reminding her that he was supporting her study of medicine and not her political and erotic activities concluded: "I am interested only in E. G. the woman—her ideas have no meaning whatever to me." Goldman wrote back with characteristic independence: "E. G., the woman and her ideas are inseparable. She does not exist for the amusement of upstarts, nor will she permit anybody to dictate to her. Keep your money" (268).

In Paris, unexpected events again shaped Goldman's future. French officials suppressed the planned anarchist conference, forcing the small group to meet clandestinely on the outskirts of Paris. She also attended a neo-Malthusian conference, which had to rotate its secret meetings because of the French government's opposition to birth control. The dozen delegates, however, shared their knowledge eagerly. For her part, Goldman was gratified to get some useful advice and felt she was well supplied with contraceptive information for her future work in the United States (173).

The Antianarchist Fever

Returning to New York in December 1900, Goldman resumed nursing and sustained a vigorous schedule of lecturing to various groups. But political events soon diverted her attention. In September 1901 Leon Czolgosz, a self-proclaimed anarchist, assassinated President William McKinley. As police throughout the country rushed to arrest radical leaders, Goldman's prominence in the anarchist movement prompted authorities to attempt to connect her with the assassination. Despite Czolgosz's denials of her involvement, she was arrested in Chicago on 10 September on suspicion of conspiracy. Intense questioning in Chicago and Czolgosz's statements in Buffalo revealed that Goldman had only a casual connection with him: he had attended a lecture of hers in Cleveland and had spoken to her without her even knowing his name or identity. Unable to establish any connection, the Chicago police released Goldman for lack of evidence (295–310).

Most anarchists repudiated Czolgosz's act publicly; even Berkman condemned it, a fact that deeply distressed Goldman. After her release, she tried to explain Czolgosz's actions to the public as the inevitable response of a sensitive individual to societal abuses. In "The Tragedy at Buffalo," written for the *Free Society*, a Chicago anarchist paper, Goldman defended Czolgosz: "I do not advocate violence; government does this, and force begets force." Czolgosz was a "soul in pain," struggling against oppressive external forces.[40] Although she opposed violence at this time to achieve social change, Goldman nonetheless understood the societal pressures that could lead others to such acts. Her own deep empathy with Czolgosz and her fellow anarchists' repudiation of him wrenched Goldman profoundly. "Our movement," she later wrote, "had lost its appeal for me" (318).

The anti-anarchist fever in the country and her disillusionment with other anarchists' failure to defend Czolgosz caused her to alter her life dramatically. Assuming a pseudonym, "Miss E. G. Smith," she resumed her nursing but curtailed her agitation for anarchism. But a few months later, she began working energetically for other causes. On tour again, Goldman lectured on behalf of the strike of American anthracite coal workers and for the victims of religious and racial oppression in Russia. She also struggled to prevent deportation of John Turner, an English anarchist on a lecture tour in the United States, under the new Federal Antianarchist Law (1903) that banned anarchists from entering the country (347–48).

During this lull in her anarchist activities, Goldman alo became a booking agent, under an alias, for Catherine Breshkovskaya, the "grandmother of the Russian Revolution," whom she had long admired (359–61). The bookings carried her into elite social circles where many of the Friends of Russian Freedom moved. This group, devoted to educating the public about the oppression of the Russian people under the czar, impressed her. Working with "Babushka," as Goldman affectionately called her, and the Friends, Goldman was determined to educate Americans about Russia. "Henceforth, I gave more time to English propaganda, not only because I wanted to bring anarchist thought to the American public but also to call attention to certain great issues in Europe. Of these the struggle for freedom in Russia was among the least understood" (358).

During this period, Goldman found that her ideas were drawing increased interest from middle-class Americans. Surprisingly, the antianarchist legislation had apparently alerted other liberal groups to the perils of such laws, and she was frequently asked to lecture to such organizations as the Brooklyn Philosophical Society and the Manhattan Liberal Club (335). Goldman's new prestige was closely related to the growth of socialism and progressivism in the United States. Not only were the progressives concerned with many of the same problems that Goldman perceived, but new radical groups were also developing in response to these abuses.[41] The time was ripe for Goldman to offer her critiques of American life to an even larger audience.

Mother Earth: A Dream Realized

After Babushka's departure, Goldman learned that the Paul Orleneff troupe, a touring Russian dramatic group, was stranded in New York. Impressed with Orleneff, she arranged performances for his troupe, acting as his agent and translator. When the troupe was immediately successful and its theater became a magnet for critics and professional actors, it expanded its performances and toured to Boston and Chicago (373–76).

This renewed contact with drama and the artistic milieu revived Goldman's interest in art as a revolutionary tool and stimulated her long-held dream of establishing a magazine "that would combine my social ideals with the young strivings in the various art forms in America" (377). Grateful for her free help, Orleneff offered to stage a special benefit performance to raise money for founding such a magazine. Circumstances forced him to do a repeat performance of Ibsen's *Ghosts* instead of a new play, which would have attracted a larger audience. Unfortunately, this performance produced only two hundred fifty of the projected thousand dollars. Nonetheless, with the slim financial base, the first sixty-four page copy of *Mother Earth* was printed in March 1906. Although Goldman had consistently written for other radical periodicals, the opportunity to edit and publish her own magazine, combining her literary interests and political theories, was exhilarating for her. Even the distressing news of her mentor Johann Most's death did not subdue her spirits for long because she had "new work to do, fascinating and absorbing" (379–81).

On 18 May 1906, Alexander Berkman was released, having served fourteen years in federal prison, often in miserable conditions. Despite her keen anticipation of resuming their sexual relationship, the years had changed both of them and they could not recapture their former intimacy. After a brief attempt to revive their love affair, they settled into a lifelong relationship as close friends, helpful colleagues, and loyal companions (384–93).

When the antianarchist fever that followed McKinley's assassination abated, Goldman pursued her extensive lecturing. Lecture tours provided funds for *Mother Earth,* which remained in a precarious financial state; they also gave her an opportunity to publicize her views on anarchism, woman's liberation, drama, free speech, and birth control. During her long absences, she left Berkman as editor of *Mother Earth,* a responsibility she hoped would raise his spirits, which had been much subdued by years of imprisonment. At the end of a spring tour in 1907, she noted that the usuallly hostile press had treated her more fairly (some were "extraordinarily decent") and that her tour had netted new subscribers as well as enough revenue from the sale of pamphlet literature to support *Mother Earth* during the summer while she attended the Anarchist Congress in Amsterdam (398).

That conference gave Goldman an opportunity to offer her own interpretation of anarchism to an international audience. Since a major topic at the conference was organization both within the movement itself and in the longed-for anarchist society, Goldman and her colleague Max Baginski addressed the tension between individualism and cooperation that was implicit in anarchist theory. They defended the individualistic anarchism represented by Dr. Stockman in Ibsen's *An Enemy of the People.* While she endorsed

Kropotkin's belief that mutual aid and cooperation were essential to the success of anarchism, Goldman insisted on the primacy of the individual and praised Ibsen's portrayal of the internal, psychological factors that produced personal revolution against societal constraints. Her passion for individualism and her belief in the power of art to vivify political ideology became hallmarks of her anarchism.

Goldman's subsequent lecture tour in Scotland and England was marred by heavy police infiltration and news of an impending legal problem in America. Her claim to American citizenship rested on her abortive marriages to Kersner, himself a naturalized citizen. Knowing this and eager to rid the United States of "Red Emma," government officials investigated Kersner's citizenship in a attempt to overturn it and, thereby, to disenfranchise Goldman.[42] Advised by friends to return promptly lest she be refused entry to the United States, she sailed to Canada and slipped across the border under the less vigilant eyes of Canadian authorities.

Return to America: The Lecture Circuit, 1908–1916

Although Goldman had lectured extensively for many years, her efforts had not garnered the funds nor the response for which she had hoped. On a fund-raising lecture tour in the spring of 1908, she met the eccentric Dr. Ben L. Reitman, "King of the Hobos," who became her inconstant lover but very effective manager.[43] Goldman averred that by his efforts "my work was lifted out of its former narrow confines." She credited Dr. Reitman, a gynecologist, with the unusual breadth and success of her 1910 tour: 120 lectures to large audiences in "many places where anarchism had never been discussed before" (469). Indeed, under Reitman's direction her lecture tours thrived, attracting larger audiences, often "packed" houses, and garnering more financial support for *Mother Earth* through the sale of subscriptions and pamphlets based on the lectures.

The success of her tours and her perception of a growing audience for her ideas caused Goldman to issue a collection of essays based on her speeches, *Anarchism and Other Essays*. Appearing in 1911, the book contained twelve essays, including an explanation of basic anarchist theory, social critiques, discussions of woman's liberation and emancipation, and an introduction to the modern drama as an expression of revolutionary themes. Through the work, Goldman hoped to reach a more serious and thoughtful audience than the one she attracted through her lectures. Reviews of her book in various periodicals indicate that to some extent she achieved her goal. The reviewer for *Life* asserted that the book "ought to be read by all so-called respectable women, and adopted as a text-book by all women's clubs throughout the country." The *Baltimore Sun* concluded that "the open-minded reader who devotes an hour or two to a perusal of *Anarchism and Other Essays,* by Emma Goldman, will put down the book with new respect for the author and perhaps also with some measure of respect for certain of her doctrines."[44]

In the years between 1908 and 1915 Goldman's tours, organized by Reitman and often lasting as long as six months, followed a similar pattern. She would leave New York in the fall or winter, swing out through Pennsylvania, Ohio, Indiana, and Illinois, up into Michigan, Wisconsin, and Minnesota, then down and west through Missouri, Kansas, and Colorado to California. After a long sojourn in California, they would move up to Oregon, Washington, and sometimes into Canada before starting east, frequently stopping in Montana or revisiting key cities on their way back to New York. The tours were very strenuous, for Goldman stayed only two or three days in most towns and typically lectured three to five times a week. Although Reitman usually arrived in a town one or two days in advance of her in order to settle final arrangements, Goldman was often denied access to lecture halls at the last moment because of police pressure. Instead of stifling her, however, such harassment seemed to increase her notoriety and her audiences.

The sites of her speeches were as varied as her topics and her audiences: labor halls, theaters, private organizations, city halls, YMCAs, hotels, and churches. Speaking sometimes in Yiddish but more often in English, Goldman ranged across social, political, economic, and literary fields. Anarchist theories, patriotism, Ferrer (an innovative Spanish educator) and modern schools, marriage and love, "Victims of Morality," "White Slavery," the danger of the increasing power of the church, Tolstoy, Ibsen, and the "Birth Strike" were all repeated topics. A common format was a debate between Goldman and a local socialist, most of whom she felt were intellectually weak opponents. For example, one circular for a lecture in San Francisco entitled "The Great Debate" announced a con-frontation between Goldman, "The Talented Anarchist," and Professor Maynard Shipley, "The Noted Socialist Lecturer and Scientist," on the resolution "that the ballot and political organization are not necessary to working class emancipation."[45] Always, Goldman relished the question and answer period at the end of her lectures because she felt she came into her own in these exchanges. The confrontation with those who opposed her views stimulated her and allowed her to become "more caustic" (213).

Every social stratum heard Goldman. Anarchists, trade unionists, and workers were attracted to some topics, while artists, doctors, lawyers, and even matrons belonging to women's clubs heard others. Goldman preferred working-class audiences and felt that her best reception was in Jewish communities. She found "respectable audiences" uncongenial. Moreover, she was contemptuous of "faddist" groups like the Intellectual Progressive Thought League of Buffalo, which she found pretentious, or the exclusive Woman's Wednesday Club in St. Louis, whose members she described as "parasitic women who think they are thinking. . . . I should not care to make a practice of speaking before the Wednesday Club audiences. Not that I fear to be contaminated. . . . It is the mental apathy of the audience at that place which is so disagreeable, like the sight of dry old bones. I could forgive the rich Americans their money; but their dullness, never."[46] Predictably, Goldman's flamboyance and her radicalism produced strong hostile reactions in some cities. Police harassment of her and her audiences, attempts to suppress *Mother Earth,* denial of halls, and even a tarring and sagebrushing of Reitman (feathers being unavailable in San Diego) marred her travels. But Goldman persisted in her lectures and in the sale of her writings, characteristically relishing the confrontations with the unenlightened.

Interestingly, she found college students and university towns to be among the least open to her ideas. She compared the rowdy students at the University of Michigan at Ann Arbor in 1910 to "escaped lunatics" and labeled them "pampered parasites" without "the backbone to fight a flea."[47] Emma delighted in her ability to turn such hostile audiences around, however. In an interview with Frank Harris for one of his volumes on contemporary figures, she recalled an experience in Ann Arbor with an exceptionally antagonistic college crowd. After describing the near bedlam that greeted her and extolling her own courage in confronting the mob, Goldman remembered, with typical vanity, that the audience soon became "intensely interested" and showed its approval at the end by giving her the college yell. "From that time I had won the heart of the students."[48]

The size of Goldman's audiences varied widely. Attendance was sharply affected by weather, local harassment (which Goldman thought promoted attendance), and the efficacy of local arrangements as well as her topic and local reputation. Frequently she spoke to large groups in full halls. Reitman's assessments of two western tours give some notion of how active and prominent Goldman was as a speaker. Between 5 January and 18 June 1910, she spoke in thirty-seven cities in twenty-five states to approximately forty thousand people. At the meetings, they sold 10,000 pieces of literature and distributed 5,000 others.[49] In six months in 1911, she visited fifty cities in eighteen states, held 150 meetings, and sold twelve hundred copies of Goldman's *Anarchism and Other Essays* and six thousand pamphlets.[50] According to her own estimate, she spoke to between fifty and seventy-five thousand people each year.[51]

Mother Earth played a central role in these tours. The periodical announced her tentative plans and solicited local persons to help organize arrangements. Moreover, Goldman reported her adventures in a regular column with various titles, such as "On the Road," "Light and Shadows in the Life of an Avante-Guard," "The Power of the Ideal," and "Agitation En Voyage." The income from the tours, in turn, provided funds for and stimulated interest in the periodical. Her lectures and the magazine were interdependent, each serving to reinforce and support the activities of the other.

When at home in New York, Goldman continued her lecturing but limited her touring radius. Philadelphia, Baltimore, Washington, Newark, Boston, Rochester, and Buffalo were among the cities most often on her home circuit. In addition, she often attended political meetings and spoke regularly in New York, frequently offering her well-received series on drama, which together with her lectures on sexual issues drew consistently large audiences.

While the wide public interest in sexual topics is perhaps predictable, the success of her drama lectures is more surprising. Of her 150 lectures in New York between October 1913 and March 1914, Goldman reported that half were devoted to drama.[52] Part of their allure came from the appeal of the literature itself. Goldman felt that audiences responded more strongly to propaganda in this guise. Her success also came from her zeal in presenting radical ideas in this indirect way. According to one observer, as Goldman spoke she burned "with the flaming ardor of an apocalytic vision" that she found expressed so eloquently in Whitman, Nietzsche, Gorky, and Hauptmann.[53] Her enthusiastic presentations spawned drama study groups in Denver and in San Francisco (493). An unexpected gift of a neat typescript of one series on drama enabled Goldman to revise the lectures and publish them in 1914 as *The Social Significance of the Modern Drama*.

During these years, Goldman lent her oratorical skills to many causes concerned with individual freedom. Denied access to halls, she agitated for free speech in New York, Chicago, and other places, helping found free speech leagues. Feeling that standard educational practices thwarted a child's natural development, she also supported the establishment of a Ferrer Center in New York. The center was dedicated to Francisco Ferrer, a Spaniard who pioneered the modern school movement in Spain and who was executed for his alleged participation in a revolutionary uprising. It soon became an active educational and social center for intellectuals and radicals in the city. Alert for cases of institutional abuse or harassment of individuals, Goldman actively defended the McNamara brothers, who were accused of dynamiting the *Los Angeles Times* in 1910. Following Berkman's lead, she agitated vigorously for Thomas J. Mooney, who had been railroaded, they felt, on charges of bombing a war preparedness parade in San Francisco in 1916 (578–79, 588). Berkman and Goldman's strenuous efforts aroused liberal opinion in Mooney's behalf and probably saved him from execution.

Her speeches on women's issues, especially her encouragement of birth control, attracted wide public attention. Although Goldman's nursing experiences led her to lecture on the theoretical need for birth control, the arrest of Margaret Sanger and her husband for distributing practical birth control information convinced Goldman that she either had to "stop lecturing on the subject or do it practical justice," by which she meant offering explicit explanations of contraceptive methods (553). At her lectures, she had already been encouraging sales of Margaret Sanger's *The Woman Rebel*, a magazine that espoused both social and sexual radicalism. Now Goldman offered two pamphlets that gave specific instructions on contraceptive methods: Sanger's *Family Limitation* and another by Reitman, who as a gynecologist was deeply committed to this cause. A New York lecture in 1916 prompted her arrest under a statute prohibiting the sale or advertisement of contraceptives, although technically she was doing neither. To get attention for the cause, Goldman used the trial and the surrounding publicity to argue for the necessity of birth control and for the freedom to distribute contraceptive information. Refusing to pay the one-hundred-dollar fine, she spent fifteen days in the Queens County jail. "One must have the consolation of an ideal to survive the forces designed to crush the prisoner. Having such an ideal, the fifteen days were a lark to me" (571). Although Goldman continued to lecture on the topic, which she felt was crucial for women, she omitted detailed instructions about contraceptive methods. Too many other issues needed her attention for her to risk further imprisonment for this cause alone. Reitman, who had agitated as vigorously as she on the subject and who had received more stringent punishment, also felt they had done their part for the cause.[54]

With the advent of war in Europe, Goldman spoke vigorously against any involvement by the United States and even against the "preparedness" being urged on all fronts. Her unpopular and outspoken resistance to what she regarded as misguided patriotism and her defense of other unpopular causes, including atheism and homosexuality, made her increasingly notorious. In a nation that by 1917 was being swept by the war fever, Goldman seemed a dangerous pariah (565–78).

The No-Conscription Conspiracy:
Anarchism on Trial

The United States's entrance into World War I dramatically altered Goldman's course. She was already a controversial figure, but her outspoken opposition to war and the draft excited further public outrage against her. Her objections to America's involvement seemed even more suspect to her critics because many of her fellow radicals had caught the war fever. Even her respected mentor Kropotkin supported the war efforts in Europe (564).

To Goldman, however, vital principles were at stake. Not only did she deplore the stupidity of patriotic carnage, but she also felt that war further enslaved workers as it enriched masters. Moreover, conscription was especially evil because it destroyed a man's freedom of ethical and political choice. Although she abhorred conscription, she felt she could not conscientiously advise men not to register, because she believed such an important matter had to be an individual choice and because, as a woman, she was not subject to the draft and could not, therefore, share the penalties for resisting. She could, however, support and aid those who chose to resist conscription. In May 1917 Goldman established the No-Conscription League to counsel those who refused conscription and organized meetings to spread the league's views (598). The cover of the June issue of *Mother Earth* summarized the league's attitude visually: it pictured a tomb with the inscription "In Memoriam—American Democracy." Although they printed 20,000 copies, far more than the usual run, the New York papers publicized these efforts even more extensively by selectively reprinting and editorializing on the material (603). The reaction of the patriotic was predictably hysterical. But Goldman vigorously pursued her activities and was gratified by the tremendous response she received. At one meeting in May, she addressed eight thousand people and was inspired by the "eagerness and determination" in her audience.[55] As police harassment of her and of the young men in her audience grew, Goldman realized that she was risking arrest or worse. In preparation for an inflammatory lecture on 14 June, she even drafted her will. Finally, she and Berkman were arrested in their offices on charges of conspiring against the draft (610–11).

The preliminary legal proceedings and the trial reflected the widespread prejudice against the defendants. The twenty-five thousand dollar bail was inordinate, real estate was refused as surety for the bond, and one friend was not permitted by her banker to cash her liberty bonds to post bail for them.[56] After the judge insisted that he would appoint an attorney if they refused to take part in the trial, Berkman and Goldman resolved to defend themselves. Realizing the chances for acquittal were slim, they used the trial as an opportunity to publicize anarchist views as well as to answer the charges against them. Despite the fact that the 18 May meeting on which the charges were based had taken place before the Conscription Law was signed by the president and although the testimony on which the charges were based was of questionable validity, the jury required only thirty-nine minutes to declare them guilty. The sentence was harsh, perhaps intended as a symbol and a warning to other opponents of conscription: two years in prison and a fine of ten thousand dollars each. The judge also recommended deportation when the sentence had been served (622). The *New York Times*

averred that the conviction of "these chronic fomentors of distur-
bance for conspiracy . . . is a public service."[57]

During the interim between the trial and their appeal, Goldman
worked arduously to prevent Berkman's extradition to California,
where he faced charges in connection with the bombing of a preparedness parade a year earlier. Although she was successful, the
repression of antiwar dissent throughout the country depressed her,
especially when *Mother Earth* was banned from the mails and was
finally forced to cease publication entirely. The quick failure of a
successor, *Mother Earth Bulletin,* ended Goldman's career as an editor-
publisher. In the midst of these problems, news of the October
revolution in Russia buoyed her spirits. She saw Lenin and Trotsky's
replacement of Kerensky, who had led the February uprising, as
"the culmination of passionate dreams and longings, the bursting
of the people's wrath against the party that it had trusted and that
had failed" (645). In her lectures and in a pamphlet entitled *The
Truth About the Bolysheviki,* Goldman sought to spread the "good
news" about Russia and its new Bolshevik leaders, a premature
enthusiasm she would later regret.

When the Supreme Court denied their appeal, she and Berkman
were transported to prison, she in Missouri and he in Atlanta.
Despite the trying conditions and the nine hours of tedious work
daily, Emma found comfort in mothering the other prisoners and
in the companionship of two fellow political prisoners: Kate Richards
O'Hare, a socialist agitator in prison for an antiwar speech, and
Gabriella Antolini, a young Italian immigrant and anarchist. Goldman also eagerly followed the unfolding events in Russia, with firm
faith in the revolution there.

Although both Goldman and Berkman raised objections to the
tactics used to secure the order for their deportation after their two
years of imprisonment in October 1919, they became victims of the
"Red Scare" sweeping the country. Because Kersner had been de-
naturalized as part of an effort to remove her citizenship, Goldman
was ordered deported despite her strenuous legal actions. Berkman,
who had never applied for citizenship, had no legal resource, but
neither feared actual deportation. Indeed, Goldman, dispirited by
the political conservatism of American society, was eager to help
with the reconstruction of Russia in the wake of the 1917 revolution.
Returning to Russia, she felt, was an opportunity to help realize
her dreams of an anarchistic society (704, 725).

Return to Russia

Although Emma Goldman returned enthusiastically to Russia and was warmly received as a brave comrade, she was soon disturbed by reports of the Bolsheviks' suppression of individual freedom. Experiences soon confirmed her fears. Suppression of dissent, harassment of anarchists, preferential treatment of those in power, and bureaucratic abuses on all sides opened her eyes to the ugliness of Bolshevik control. Seeking confirmation about her fears for the revolution from friends like Maxim Gorky and John Reed, the American expatriate and well-known radical journalist, Goldman was appalled at their defense of what was happening as a necessary precedent to a free state, and she rejected their argument that the proposed ends justified the temporary means (740–42). Even her oldest ally Berkman charged her with being only an armchair theorist of revolution, naive about the sometimes brutal realities. But reports of people like Maria Spiridonovna, who had suffered for the revolution under the czar and were then persecuted by the Bolsheviks, persuaded Goldman that the new regime was more a change of masters for the masses than a movement toward an ideal, free society (802–4).

Convinced of the state's abuses, Goldman refused any practical or symbolic employment that would support it. Instead, determined not to remain idle, she became part of a team of researchers traveling through Russia to gather artifacts and information for a Museum of the Revolution. Because Goldman distinguished the revolution of 1917 from the subsequent Bolshevik government, she could participate in this research without compromising her beliefs. The travel also gave her a chance to evaluate the situation throughout the country and to meet the masses in whom she still had faith. Firsthand knowledge deepened her opposition to the Bolsheviks (782–800).

Finally, the regime's brutal treatment of the sailors at Kronstadt, who had aided the Bolsheviks in overthrowing Kerensky, became the deciding incident. When the government used military force against the sailors, who were demanding free speech and a free press, both Goldman and Berkman were completely disillusioned; they resolved to leave Russia (886). But since their friction with authorities had made them suspect, they knew that a request to leave would accentuate doubts about their political loyalties and raise fears that they would repudiate the Bolsheviks to a worldwide audience.

Consequently, they were both relieved when an invitation to an anarchist congress in Berlin provided the pretext for an exit visa. Despite sincere sadness at leaving friends, the two set out in what was to become a lifelong exile and an unending search for a new home (923–27).

The Beginning of Exile

Settling temporarily in Stockholm, Goldman and Berkman decided to enlighten those who still supported the Bolsheviks by writing candidly of their experiences. When their first article appeared in a Swedish anarchist paper, the prime minister notified them that any such publications in the future would be "inadvisable" (934). With the help of her niece, Goldman, who felt particularly conscience-stricken about her enthusiastic public defense of the Bolsheviks, tried unsuccessfully to place an article on the persecuted revolutionary Maria Spiridonovna in an American periodical. Finally, the *New York World* offered her $2,100 for a series on her experiences. Although Berkman objected that the capitalistic press was the wrong channel through which to relay her message to the workers, Goldman prepared a seven-part exposé that was published in March and April 1922 (936–37). She admitted to one correspondent that she also had scruples about writing for the *New York World,* but indicated that she felt compelled to report her experiences, which had left scars "upon my soul . . . which I will never, never be able to make known."[58]

After repeated delays, Goldman was finally granted a German visa and she joined Berkman, who had already emigrated to Berlin. With a $1,750 advance from an American publisher, she began a book chronicling her Russian experience (944). In writing, Goldman relied heavily on Berkman's detailed journal of their joint sojourn. Her use of his notes, her incorporation of them into her work, and her demands on him to edit the book postponed his efforts on a similar project and finally dismayed him. Although his book *Bolshevik Myth* appeared soon after hers and was judged superior by many critics, Berkman resented Goldman's insensitivity.[59]

Doubleday and Page altered her title from the neutral *My Two Years in Russia* to the more provocative *My Disillusionment in Russia* when publishing her book, a characterization that she felt misrepresented her views. In addition, the last twelve chapters, including an afterword clarifying her political theories, were lost in the transition from the intermediary to the publisher and were omitted from the first edition. To her dismay, few critics noted that the initial volume was strangely truncated although several reviewed it. At her insistence, Doubleday brought out the missing twelve chapters as a separate volume, again misleadingly titled *My Further Disillusionment in Russia* (954).[60] The work that chronicled her experiences and repudiated the Bolsheviks as perverters of the revolution of 1917 had little impact among those sympathetic to the cause.

Forced out of Germany in July 1924 by hostile reactions to her book, Goldman turned to England, a country that seemed to offer the only promising avenue for her continued anarchist agitation. But her efforts were frustrating. The anarchist movement that existed in England was lethargic, and Goldman was uncertain about how to stimulate interest. Her indictment of the Bolsheviks alienated most London liberals despite Rebecca West's efforts on her behalf. Predictably, socialists and labor politicians rejected what they regarded as her "reactionary" views (968). Moreover, the British Trade Union delegation, which returned from Russia impressed with the successes of the revolution, issued a report that directly contradicted Goldman's depictions (971). Although Goldman tried to answer their "whitewash," liberal support for her dwindled further. Only Rebecca West remained friendly, writing a preface for and helping her to publish a British edition of *My Disillusionment in Russia* (975).

Frustrated both by the reception of her evidence against the Bolsheviks and by her inability to speak out on British social problems because of her status as an alien, Goldman used her familiarity with recent developments in drama and her connections with the Provincetown Playhouse in America to lecture on drama. She even began extensive research in the British Museum for a projected book on Russian drama (978–79). Although she thought the audiences were receptive and intelligent, Goldman made very little money for her efforts.

In June 1925, to secure the protection of British citizenship, she married James Colton, a Welsh coalminer and longtime anarchist friend. Since England had proven disappointing financially and professionally, Goldman departed for the milder climate of St. Tropez, where friends had purchased her a small cottage. The *American*

Mercury had supplied her with an advance to write an essay on her early mentor Johann Most (981). For the first time, Goldman was forced to worry about establishing and maintaining her financial independence. Unfortunately, this cloud lingered for the rest of her life, for she often had to help an ailing Berkman as well as supply her own modest needs (982). She hoped to publish her book on Russian drama and undertake a Canadian lecture tour to raise funds. Just as her work on the book was going well, however, unexpected economic conditions in England forced the publisher to withdraw support. Finally, only loans from old American friends provided the financing for her projected Canadian tour (985–86).

The tour was moderately successful. Due to the inexperience of the sponsors and to poor organization, her first lectures in Montreal drew small crowds. But the help of C. R. Reade, a reporter for the *Toronto Star,* improved attendance, and her stops in Winnipeg and Edmonton drew larger crowds. Her schedule was rigorous: she lectured fifteen times in one week, three times on some days (989). Given a brief rest in Toronto with funds and a secretary provided by friends, Goldman prepared a new series of twenty lectures, which proved quite popular.

In early 1928 she returned to Montreal to sail for France. Goldman felt satisfied with her work and more confident about the future than at any time since she had left for Russia full of expectations of an imminent anarchist state. "In fifteen months I had raised over thirteen hundred dollars for the political fund, some money for the fight to rescue Sacco and Vanzetti, and for similar causes. I had paid my debts, amounting to twelve hundred dollars, and I had enough left to cover my return passage, aside from the new fund for my autobiography. I was returning to France, to lovely Saint-Tropez and my enchanting little cottage to write my life. My life— I had lived in its heights and its depths, in bitter sorrow and ecstatic joy, in black despair and fervent hope. I had drunk the cup to the last drop. I had lived my life. Would I had the gift to paint the life I had lived" (993).

The Final Years

Unfortunately, Goldman's final years at Bon Espirit, the cottage in France near St. Tropez purchased by her friends, were not free of troubles. Berkman was settled in an uneasy, insecure exile nearby in Nice; with his editorial assistance she completed her lengthy autobiography in early 1931. The two-volume work sold for $7.50 despite her protest that the price was beyond the means of the workers whom she envisioned as her proper audience. Although circulation reports and endorsements by librarians and critics suggested a wide public appeal for her memoirs, few copies were sold. Goldman was bitterly disappointed that it generated no funds for her and Berkman.[61]

Lecture tours to Copenhagen, Oslo, and Stockholm invigorated her, despite her growing apprehensions about Hitler's rise and the worsening conditions in Europe. With Europe increasingly closed to her, Goldman hoped to return to the United States and Canada for tours. Through the efforts of Mable Carver Crouch, a well-known liberal, with the support of John Dewey, Sherwood Anderson, and Sinclair Lewis, and with the encouragment of the American Civil Liberties Union (ACLU), Goldman was permitted to visit the United States in 1934 for ninety days provided she limit her talks to drama and literature.[62] At first she balked at any restrictions, unwilling to constrain her expression of anarchist ideas and arguing that literature without its social context was meaningless. Roger Baldwin, head of the ACLU, who was handling official negotiations for her return, urged her to accept the proviso, pointing out that she could lecture on other topics once admitted.[63] She acquiesced and arrived in New York on 1 February 1934.

Her tour was hectic and controversial, but not financially successful. Because she needed funds to support herself and Berkman, she may have regretted her rejection of an offer to appear on the vaudeville circuit for two thousand dollars a week. She blamed her manager's extravagance and unwise planning for the tour's financial failure. Richard Drinnon locates another factor in the changed radicalism in America in the 1930s, which made her ideas look at best "hopelessly old-fashioned."[64] Goldman's rejection of both fascism and communism, the most popular radical views of the day, probably limited her audiences. Despite the disappointing public response, Goldman thrived on exposure to the American scene. Shortly after leaving, she wrote to Berkman that in America "there is still the spirit of adventure, there is something refreshing and stimulating in the air. . . . America brings out adventure, innovations, experimental daring which, except for Russia, no European country does. And it is this surcharged, electric, and dynamic at-

mosphere which permeates its writers, poets, and dramatists. You'd
rub your eyes if you could see some of the plays now given on the
American stage."[65] When the Commission of Immigration refused
to approve a longer stay, she sailed despondently back to France.
In a letter to Roger Baldwin after her return, Goldman acknowledged that the trip had made her realize that she had never accli-
matized herself to any place in Europe, that she remained deeply
rooted to the United States, but would, unfortunately, be forced to
"remain an alien abroad for the rest of my life."[66]

In France Goldman and Berkman faced severe problems, and
Berkman was despondent. Constantly intimidated by French officials who threatened to terminate his visa, he worked as a translator
and ghostwriter for meager commissions. In near desperation, the
two even tried setting up a tenting camp on her property, but only
two campers appeared. Goldman helped Berkman when she could,
although she was chronically short of funds.[67] Tension between
Goldman and a young woman companion of Berkman's further
complicated matters. Despite their problems their relationship en-
dured. Goldman sent Berkman a note on his birthday that expressed
quite directly her feelings toward him:

As a greeting to your sixty-fifth birthday it is fitting that I should tell
you the secret of my life. It is that the one treasure I have rescued from
my long and bitter struggle is my friendship for you. . . . I know of no
other value, whether in people or achievements, than your presence in my
life and the love and affection you have roused. . . . No one ever was so
rooted in my being, so ingrained in my every fiber, as you have been and
are to this day. Men have come and gone in my long life. But you, my
dearest will remain forever. . . . I know that the only loss that would
matter would be to lose you or your friendship.[68]

Despite her warm reassurance, Berkman's spirits sank still lower.
Depressed by financial worries and ill health, Berkman shot himself
in June 1936. Devastated and alone, Goldman saw no future for
herself.[69]

A request later that year from Augustine Souchy, secretary of a
Spanish anarcho-syndicalist group, for her to assist the Spanish workers in their rebellion, promised a new outlet for her energies. Dis-
mayed at the violence of the revolution in Spain, Goldman was still
impressed with the group's spirit and with their constructive activities in agriculture and collectivized factories.[70] She was most ex-

hilarated by their experimental school, based on libertarian principles. In London she worked with great zeal but little success as the group's propagandist. Organizing support groups for emigré women and children, arranging exhibits of Catalonian art, and showing Spanish films raised little money. Although she opposed the Spanish anarchists' participation in the government and their cooperation with the Communists, she continued to seek aid for them, even traveling to Canada to raise funds. To the end she hoped that the Spanish uprising would provide a symbolic and practical alternative to the perversion of the revolution by the Bolshevik in Russia.

On 17 February 1940 while seeking money in Canada for the Spanish Revolutionaries, Goldman suffered a paralyzing stroke. On May 14 she died. At the request of friends, the United States government permitted the return of her body to Chicago to be buried at Waldheim Cemetery, appropriately close to the graves of the Haymarket strikers.[71] Harry Weinberger, her longtime friend and lawyer, accurately said of her at her memorial service: "She was tireless; she was fearless; she never compromised; liberty was always her theme; liberty was always her dream; liberty was always her goal. Emma Goldman, we welcome you back to America; you will live forever in the hearts of your friends and the story of your life will live as long as the stories are told of women and men of courage and idealism."[72]

Chapter Two
Philosophical and Political Essays

Anarchism . . . the great, surging living truth.
—"Anarchism: What It Really Stands For"

"Anarchism, the great leaven of thought," stimulated Emma Goldman's writing and permeated her perceptions of people, events, and literature. She was not, however, an original theorist. A contemporary, Hutchins Hapgood, who heard many of her speeches, felt her ideas "were too simple and too orthodox as a faithful expression of the traditional revolution of the working class" to be interesting.[1] Charles A. Madison characterized her as "a faithful disciple of Bakunin and Kropotkin."[2] Goldman's works primarily synthesize and adapt the views of other, more original thinkers, as her frequent references to Proudhon, Bakunin, Stirner, and Kropotkin reveal. Her greatest achievements were as an interpreter and as a propagandist of anarchism.

Roots of Goldman's Anarchism:
European Theorists

To understand Goldman's writings on anarchism, we must know something of the history of the anarchist movement and of the stages of her development as an anarchist thinker. As an immigrant and under the tutelage of Johann Most, himself a European refugee, Goldman was more influenced by European anarchists than by native-born American theorists. Although she identified Peter Kropotkin publicly as her primary mentor, she also derived insights from earlier writers, including Pierre-Joseph Proudhon, Michael Bakunin, Max Stirner, and Friedrich Nietzsche. Each man contributed important, distinctive elements to her thinking, and her attempted amalgamation of them colored her speaking and writing, sometimes compelling her into confusing inconsistencies.

Although we can trace modern anarchist ideas back to include William Godwin (1756–1836), the prominent English libertarian philosopher, writer, and founding father of anarchism, the movement is largely a development of the middle and late nineteenth century.[3] Thus, Goldman entered the movement in its most dynamic period. Despite differences in emphasis and approaches to achieving social change, the anarchists shared an opposition to centralized government that distinguished them from the socialists and finally made them opponents of Karl Marx, with whom early anarchists found much in common. As a group, the anarchists favored abolition of centralized government and advocated some form of communal or collectivized economic arrangement to combat the exploitative evils of capitalism. To differing degrees, they insisted on the importance of the individual and on personal freedom from any restraints.

Proudhon (1819–1865), a self-educated French printer, was the first to adopt the label *anarchist* for the views he advanced. In 1840 in a pamphlet entitled *What Is Property?* he answered that "property is theft" and expressed the individualist doctrines that became the foundation of later anarchist theory. Proudhon did not object to a person's control over the products of his or her own labor, but instead decried ownership of the means of production by anyone other than laborers or labor collectives. Objecting to government as an infringement on personal freedom, he advocated workers' associations devoted to mutual credit among producers as the ideal economic mechanism to replace the nation-state.[4] Although he initially found much in common with Karl Marx, whom he knew in Paris, Proudhon rejected the statism implicit in Marx's ideas. His antipathy for the state and his support of workers' associations as an alternative to capitalism and socialistic communism became the hallmarks of later anarchism. His assertion that "property is theft" became a popular slogan of radicals of the day, which Goldman incorporated into her primary essay explaining anarchism.[5]

If Proudhon provided the theoretical bases for her views, fellow Russian Michael Bakunin (1814–1876) provided a model of the revolutionary activist. Bakunin, born to well-educated and politically liberal parents, roamed through Europe in pursuit of both intellectual companionship and revolutionary activity. In Paris in the 1840s, where he knew both Proudhon and Marx, he agreed with them that earlier revolutions, including the English, the French, and the American, had been only partially successful because they had achieved political change but not fundamental social change.[6] Bakunin, who concurred with Marx's assessment of him as a "sentimental idealist," was eager to foment and participate in revolutionary activity in any locale.[7] In contrast to Proudhon's "mutualism," which rejected revolutionary violence and emphasized the individual worker as the basic economic unit, Bakunin's "collectivism" supported public ownership of land, services, and means of production. Bakunin saw the group of workers, the collective—not the individual—as the central focus.[8] Bakunin's views gained wide currency among radical groups in the United States, which often tended toward labor organization as the mechanism for social change. Goldman's tacit support for labor unions, which later separated her from Most, reflects this tenet of Bakunin's theories. Devoted to the overthrow of oppressive institutional power and willing to leave the details of government after the revolution to others, Bakunin became a paradigm for the radical activist. Goldman admired him as a personality. His zest for living and his deep involvement in concrete revolutionary activity particularly impressed her. She preferred his direct political agitation to the speculations of armchair theorists who had little contact with reality.[9]

In addition to her interest in political and social issues, Goldman was always deeply concerned for the individual and for the principle of self-determination. Thus, she was never fully sympathetic with the focus on the mass, which characterized many revolutionary thinkers. While Bakunin and Proudhon emphasized the need for social revolution and urged some form of collective organization to correct economic abuses, Max Stirner, a German schoolteacher, stressed the desirability of individual freedom and personal growth, themes that resonated with Goldman and later permeate her writing. Moreover, her efforts to reconcile Stirner's commitment to individualism with the collectivism of other theorists became a hallmark of her particular version of anarchism and produced significant tensions in her thinking.

Stirner, whom George Woodcock labels "the egoist" among anarchists, focused on the individual "who realizes himself in conflict with the collectivity."[10] In *The Ego and His Own* (1843), Stirner exalts the individual will and passion and castigates all the artificial constructions, including myth and philosophy, that obscure a person's sense of self. Because the state by its very nature prizes the collective rather than the individual, it is always the enemy of the egoist. This individualism was tremendously appealing to Goldman, who always insisted on the primacy of the individual. The concept of the enlightened individual as the shaper of events excited her and came to define her version of anarchism in contrast to those who perceived the mass as the source of revolutionary authority. Later she found reinforcement of this view in the works of Nietzsche, which she discovered during her sojourn in Vienna in 1895–1896. In her autobiography, Goldman recalled her desire to read all of Nietzsche's works because "the magic of his language, the beauty of his vision, carried me to undreamed-of heights." Her enthusiasm for Nietzsche's individualism and his condemnation of religion led her to overlook or excuse other less anarchistic features in his philosophy. For example, she explained his aristocratic leanings as being "neither of birth nor of the purse" but "of the spirit," and she ignored his mistrust of women entirely. [11] Although Goldman prized the revolutionary spirit she perceived in the Russian people and sympathized with the plight of the oppressed masses, she consistently castigated the blindness and inertia of other groups and looked instead to inspired individuals to instigate radical reforms. Consequently, any revolution or regime that penalized the individual or repressed personal liberty in the name of progress was unacceptable to her.

In 1864, sensing a need for some form of organization to allow them to discuss their views and promulgate their doctrines, the followers of Proudhon and Bakunin established the International Workingman's Association, the First International, in which Marx participated. But personal and philosophical differences between Marx and Bakunin led to the rupture of the group in 1872. Left without any official international network, the anarchist movement survived in scattered groups. Surprisingly, despite its disorganization, anarchist ideology flourished between 1880 and 1890, largely through the energetic efforts and personal charisma of Peter Kropotkin. [12]

Although born into a privileged Russian family, Kropotkin (1842–1921) did not follow the comfortable path his family envisioned for him. [13] His experiences investigating the penal system in Siberia as a military aide-de-camp cemented his liberal leanings, but he despaired of achieving significant reforms under contemporary conditions. Abandoning a promising military career because of his scruples, Kropotkin devoted himself to geographic exploration, in which he achieved a distinguished record. Finally, however, his conscience forced him back to concern for social change. Working first as an agitator and activist, he drifted into writing and editing. Gradually, he developed a theory of anarchist communism that emphasized human beings' natural leaning toward social responsibility. Applying the scientific theory of evolution to social change in his theory of "mutual aid," Kropotkin highlighted the basis in nature for cooperation rather than for competition as a means of human development and improvement. His vision of a society comprised of collectives based on the principle of voluntary cooperation was inspiring, especially to Goldman, who resisted any forced associations even though she never fully shared his optimistic assessment of the masses and felt his views to be somewhat naive and unrealistic.[14]

Goldman's Development as an Anarchist

Even before Goldman learned of these theorists, she had absorbed radical ideas from various sources. Her contacts as a girl with clandestine reading groups in St. Petersburg, which resisted the repressive tactics of the czar's state censoring, had built on her innate disposition and childhood perceptions. Her traumatic experiences in the factories of Rochester had made her fully aware of the abuses of capitalism and receptive to calls for change. Because she found the worker's life so intolerably constrained, Goldman saw a need for radical action. The Haymarket incident not only dramatized the oppression she had experienced firsthand, but the unfair legal treatment of the innocent anarchists and the biased, unsympathetic press depictions of them aroused her sympathies for them and their movement. In every sense, the young woman who returned to New York after twice divorcing her husband and having lived the problems of the workers was ripe for induction into and indoctrination about the anarchist movement.

The almost happenstance appearance of Johann Most as her mentor was also crucial in Goldman's development. His forceful personality and attraction to her smoothed the way for her entrance into anarchist activities. Under his tutelage, she expanded her reading beyond radical periodicals and became acquainted with the prominent anarchist theorists. Perhaps equally important, Most's enthusiasm for art and drama and his willingness to make sacrifices in order to afford a ticket to an opera led Goldman to see these experiences as appropriate and productive activities, even for a person vehemently committed to a political cause. Stirred by Johann Most's activist zeal, she even embraced his notion of political violence as an appropriate revolutionary tool. But his autocratic personality distressed her personally, and soon she found herself disagreeing with his views. Particularly, Goldman was more supportive of trade unions than he, and she resented his somewhat condescending attitude toward her as a woman. As a result, she was drawn to Most's rival, Joseph Peukert.[15] If Peukert lacked Most's charisma, his periodical, *Autonomie,* and his supporters espoused a version of anarchism that highlighted the freedom of the individual and the independence of groups, two views that appealed to her.

Throughout the 1890s as she pursued her study of anarchist texts and continued her involvement in the movement's activities, Goldman deepened her commitment to the individualism propounded by Stirner and to the concept of collectives based on voluntary cooperation urged by Kropotkin. During this period, her increasing familiarity with literature provided a new element in her thinking. Her deeper exposure to the works of Nietzsche, Ibsen, Strindberg, and Hauptmann in Vienna in 1895 and 1896 led her to appreciate what she regarded as their artistic depiction of her individualistic theories of anarchism. She began to argue for the close connection between art and anarchism and to see literature as an important tool for social change.

As she emerged as a leader, Goldman spoke regularly on social issues as well on anarchist theory, writing occasionally for periodicals like the *Firebrand,* which later became the *Free Society,* and *Lucifer,* which developed into the *American Journal of Eugenics.*[16] Goldman's exposure to the *Lucifer* helped shape her strong commitment to radical woman's liberation, a view not shared by all anarchists.[17] Edited by Moses Harman, *Lucifer* was a periodical dedicated to freethinking in all dimensions of life, and it frequently expressed views about the importance of woman's liberation to the larger radical cause, which Goldman found compelling.[18] Her attendance at Freud's lectures in Vienna had undoubtedly promoted this development because she wrote: "For the first time I grasped the full significance of sex repression and its effect on human thought and action." When she met Harman, whom she had long admired as "the courageous champion of free motherhood and woman's economic and sexual emancipation," she reported that they spent the

entire evening "discussing problems affecting woman and her emancipation."[19] In addition to her own speaking and writing, Goldman
continued to read widely in the radical press as well as in literature.
As a result of these divergent forces and experiences, by the end of
the 1890s she had largely formulated the theories she was to follow
until her disillusioning experiences in postrevolutionary Russia.[20]

As Goldman struggled to clarify her own views on anarchism
during the 1890s, the movement was also attempting to organize
its efforts and establish an international network. After their ex-
pulsion from the First International by the Marxists in 1872, anarchists had attempted to organize their own international meeting,
but police harassment had balked their attempts. The aborted meeting that Goldman tried to attend in Paris in 1900 was typical of
the problems they confronted.[21] The first successful effort at an
international conference in Amsterdam in 1907 came at a propitious
time for Goldman. Her extensive lecturing had helped her hone her
thinking, and in her travels both at home and abroad she had talked
with many of the leading radicals of the time. She was thus prepared
to express her views confidently and forcefully.

In her presentation to the Amsterdam conference, coauthored with
Max Baginski, Goldman insisted on the individualistic element in
anarchism. Because both she and Baginski were admirers of Ibsen's
works, they used Dr. Stockmann from *An Enemy of the People* as the
paradigm of the dedicated and socially responsible individual who
could lead the way to important social change almost single-hand-
edly. Drawing heavily on Nietzsche and Stirner, she admitted that
cooperation and collective action were essential to achieve social
change. She averred, however, that individualism must precede such
organization because no healthy, dynamic organization could "result
from the combination of mere non-entities. It must be composed
of self-conscious, intelligent individualities."[22] Although Goldman
did not articulate the feminist strain of her views at the conference,
she was pleased with her efforts, which a recent scholar believes
constitute "her nearest approach to an original contribution to anarchist theory."[23]

With the founding of *Mother Earth* in 1906, Goldman had a
convenient forum for conveying her ideas to people she could not
reach frequently with her lecture and for cementing her views among
her followers. Her years as editor and publisher, from 1906 to 1917,

were prolific. No longer dependent on the ephemeral spoken word, Goldman could adapt her lectures into essays that readers could peruse carefully. The written word, she had come to feel, was more effective than oratory in achieving social change, therefore, she used *Mother Earth* to urge her ideas.[24] Although most of her essays in *Mother Earth* were based closely on her speeches, her column reporting her lectures and her editorial notes accentuate the theories she developed in longer pieces. Moreover, the editorial process of selecting, recruiting, and publishing essays allowed her to express her preferences more indirectly. The periodical as a whole, then, became an expression of her attitudes.

In 1910 Goldman adapted several of her lectures into essays and published them as *Anarchism and Other Essays*. Arguing that the written word allowed a "more intimate" contact between writer and reader than speeches did, she added: "It is this certainty which has induced me to gather in one volume my ideas on various topics of individual importance. They represent the mental and soul struggles of twenty-one years—the conclusions derived after many changes and inner revisions."[25]

Goldman was concerned both with educating her audience about anarchism and with pointing up the problems and abuses she perceived in society as it was then structured. Thus, her essays fall into two general classes: those that articulate her anarchist doctrines directly and those that discuss social issues from her ideological perspective. This division is one of emphasis, for all her essays treat anarchist themes. By first examining her more theoretical essays, we can better understand the criteria she employed to scrutinize society and its problems.

Because the essays overlap and are often repetitious, treatment of each work is unnecessarily redundant. Instead, this discussion will focus on the main tenets of her theories and concentrate on one or two primary essays that illustrate her views. This approach both clarifies her ideas and preserves some of the flavor of the individual works. Major aspects of Goldman's theory are: (1) her definition and defense of anarchism contained in the lead essay from her *Anarchism and Other Essays*, "Anarchism: What It Really Stands For"; (2) her indictment of religion, provided in two essays she published in *Mother Earth* on Christianity and atheism; (3) her individualism, as she offered it in "Minorities versus Majorities," the second essay in her *Anarchism;* and (4) her reaction to and analysis of the Russian Revolution, both before and after her exile, which she treated in various essays and in the afterword to *My Disillusionment in Russia.*

Anarchism as a Liberator of the Human Spirit: "Anarchism: What It Really Stands For"

Goldman's anarchism was essentially libertarianism, for she urged total individual freedom and opposed any centralized government. Both democratic capitalism with its majority rule and socialism with its highly centralized power were repugnant to her because both limited the individual's control over his or her affairs. The greatest personal fulfillment and growth, she believed, occurred when individuals were absolutely free to pursue their own directions.

As the title "Anarchism: What It Really Stands For" suggests, Goldman hoped to correct the reader's misapprehensions about anarchist theories. The poem by John Henry Mackay with which she introduces the essay indicates her approach. After alluding to the misunderstanding about anarchy—"Ever reviled, accursed, ne'er understood,"—her essay castigates those who have not sought to understand the concept and argues that anarchism will blossom in the future "when each at least unto himself shall waken." Finally, it summarizes the anarchist position: "I am an Anarchist! Wherefore I will / Not rule, and also ruled I will not be!"[26]

Using Mackay's poem as her framework, Goldman argues that the misunderstandings and fears about anarchism are typical of the "Old's" resistance to "every new idea heralding the approach of a brighter dawn." To counter these misperceptions she proposes first to answer what she calls the two major objections to anarchism—its impracticality and its destructiveness—then to discuss its true nature. After simply asserting that anarchism is practical because it can build and sustain new growth—her unsupported tests of feasibility—she refutes the charge that it is destructive with an effective, if inelegant and confused, metaphor: "Anarchism, whose roots, as it were, are part of nature's forces, destroys not healthy tissue, but parasitic growths that feed on the life's essence of society. It is merely clearing the soil from weeds and sagebrushes that it may eventually bear healthy fruit" (49–50).

With these objections met, Goldman offers a definition of anarchism to avoid taxing her reader's "brain capacity" (a typical bit of her sarcasm): "Anarchism: The philosophy of a new social order based on liberty unrestricted by man-made law; the theory that all forms of government rest on violence, and are therefore wrong and harmful, as well as unnecessary" (50). Then she moves to an explanation of humankind's current circumstance.

Most problems arise, Goldman thinks, because two forces have worked historically on humans: the impulse toward individualism (which Stirner had articulated) and the instinct toward social organization (which Kropotkin prized). Primitive humans, uncertain of their power to control their environment, turned to religion, to society, and later to the state for protection and assistance. These human-made entities encouraged continued reliance on them by emphasizing human insecurities. Insisting that individual "man is nothing, the powers everything," these religious, cultural, and political institutions thwarted the natural human urge toward individualism and self-awareness (51).

The precedence of social institutions over individuals also produced an unnecessarily bitter conflict between the two instincts, both of which could make important contributions to human existence. Individualism promoted growth, aspiration, and self-realization; the social instinct encouraged mutual helpfulness and produced common well-being. There is no conflict between individualism and the social instincts, Goldman argues, "any more than there is between the heart and the lungs: the one the receptacle of a precious life essence, the other the repository of the element that keeps the essence pure and strong. The individual is the heart of society, conserving the essence of the social life, society is the lungs which are distributing the element to keep the life essence—that is, the individual—pure and strong" (50). In making society primary, humans had created an artificial tension between their individualistic and their social instincts. Anarchism could restore the lost balance by affirming that religion, the social order, and the nationalistic state were the creations of human beings rather than their masters. "Anarchism is the great liberator of man from the phantoms that have held him captive; it is the arbiter and pacifer of the two forces for individual and social harmony" (52). Goldman insists that anarchism, in reasserting the primacy of the individual, will unleash creative human development by removing artificial societal constraints.

Three societal forces were the primary foes of the freedom Goldman advocates: "Religion, the dominion of the human mind; Property, the dominion of human needs; and Government, the dominion of human conduct, represent the stronghold of man's enslavement and all the horrors it entails" (53). These forces derive their power and control from their early roots in human ignorance and fear.

In a brief but scathing paragraph, Goldman outlines her attitude toward religion. Arguing that the "black monster" of religion "humiliates and degrades" human souls, she contends that God had created "a kingdom so despotic, so tyrannical, so cruel, so terribly exacting that naught but gloom and tears and blood have ruled the world since gods began." Only when humankind casts off its "mental fetters" can it be free of the "the dominion of darkness, the greatest obstacle to all progress" (53).

While religion shackles people's minds, the private control of property denies them the right to satisfy their needs and deforms them psychologically. In an industrialized, capitalistic society, she argues, workers cannot enjoy the fruits of their labor nor earn enough to satisfy their needs. "Property is robbery," Goldman insists, quoting Proudhon. "Yes, but without risk and danger to the robber. Monopolizing the accumulated efforts of man, property has robbed him of his birthright, and has turned him loose a pauper and an outcast." America's boasts of great national wealth are both hollow and wrong, she contends; in fact, its citizens are "wretchedly poor" because the riches are concentrated in the hands of a few. In a typically melodramatic image, Goldman says that workers are forced to "live in squalor, in filth, in crime, with hope and joy gone, a homeless, soilless army of human prey." Further, she notes that the cost of production in terms of human life and injury will finally bankrupt the capitalistic economy because "the returns to the masses, who help create the wealth, are getting ever smaller" (54).

The psychological impact of private property is even more vicious than its economic effects. Not only are workers transformed into wage slaves, but they are alienated from their own productions. The products of their labor confront them, as Marx argued, as alien, hostile objects. "Fatal is the crime of turning the producer into a mere particle of a machine with less will and decision than his master of steel and iron. Man is robbed not merely of the products of his labor, but of the power of free initiative, of originality, and the interest in, or desire for, the things he is making" (54–55). Workers become alienated automatons, deprived of the joys of meaningful work and deadened by the monotony of their routines. With no outlet for self-expression, they lose that creative spark and joy in living that Goldman thinks are the most positive characteristics of human nature.

As a panacea for the sickness of private property, Goldman envisions an economic arrangement consisting of "voluntary production and distributive association, gradually developing into free communism." At all times, however, the individual must be "free to choose the mode of work, the conditions of work, and the freedom to work" (55–56). She barely sketches her alternative to capitalism in this essay, but provides a fuller model in her essays on syndicalism, which appeared in *Mother Earth*. In contrast to trade unionism, which works within the capitalistic wage system to improve conditions, syndicalism repudiates that inherently antagonistic arrangement and urges "free development of production for the benefit of all humanity." Workers' cooperatives would not only control production, but would also educate and prepare workers for their role in a free society. The societies developed by French syndicalists to secure work for the unemployed and to foster the spirit of mutual assistance were to be, she stresses, models for the universal expansion of such cooperation. To secure this radical economic restructuring, syndicalism advocates three coercive tactics: sabotage, direct action, and the general strike. Sabotage entails the destruction or disabling of means of production or distribution. Direct action involves any method of protesting or thwarting capitalistic abuses including, for example, mishandling of merchandise to destroy its value or employing bureaucratic technicalities to slow down shipment. The general strike is a spontaneous action by workers to halt production and distribution entirely. These techniques are desirable because they assert the economic power of the worker and touch "capitalism in its most vital spot, the pocket." For Goldman, syndicalism is "the economic expression of Anarchism."[27]

In short, Goldman contends that the capitalistic system has perverted and crushed individualism. By demeaning the worker economically and psychologically, capitalism has concentrated property in the hands of the few, which has stifled humanity. Socialism, which concentrates the power in the hands of the state, is not a satisfactory alternative, however. Only a communistic society, achieved in part by syndicalism, can provide a radically healthy economic environment for free human development.

Having castigated the tyranny of religion and the inequities of capitalism, Goldman turns her attention to "the greatest foe of all social equality," which is, of course, the nation-state. Defining it as "organized authority or statutory law," Goldman repudiates any form of centralized civil government. With its structure of human-made laws, the state fetters the individual and invades his or her most private affairs. Because it always places external dictates about personal matters, the state abuses the individual in the name of the mass. Quoting Emerson, Goldman argues, "All government in essence is tyranny" (56).

Because the state seeks its own perpetuation and has as its aim the "absolute subordination of the individual," its keynote is injustice. While ordaining, judging, condemning, and punishing the most trivial offenses to maintain itself, the state commits the greatest of all offenses, the destruction of human freedom. Citing Bakunin, Goldman notes that the state is "synonymous with the surrender of the liberty of the individual." It is, she adds with a characteristically vivid image, "the altar of political freedom and like the religious altar, it is maintained for the purpose of human sacrifice" (57).

In agreement with almost all "modern thinkers," Goldman asserts that the state is "necessary *only* to maintain or protect property and monopoly. It has proven efficient in that function only." With this thesis behind her, she then answers those who claim that the state is founded on natural law and that it serves useful functions in society (57–58). A natural law is, in Goldman's definition, "that factor in man which asserts itself freely and spontaneously without any external force, in harmony with the requirements of nature." In light of this definition, she argues, the state could not be derived from natural law because it distributes economic benefits unfairly between the workers and the owners. By doing so, it destroys the basis for any "solidarity of interests" that must underlie any harmonious social order. Its functioning, in essence, is theoretically antithetical to natural law (58–59).

On a more pragmatic level, Goldman argues that the state is ineffectual, unproductive, and unjust. Although the state is constituted supposedly to control antisocial behavior, it "has come to an absolute standstill in coping with crime. It has failed utterly to destroy or even minimize the horrible scourge of its own creation." Relying on force and violence to enforce its intrusive regulations, the state is "itself the greatest criminal, breaking every written and natural law, stealing in the form of taxes, killing in the form of war and capital punishment." Goldman asserts, indeed, that the inequitable and abusive social system makes crime inevitable and that the punishments meted out for such petty offense further demoralize and demean human beings. She agrees with Peter Kropotkin that "the entire apparatus of prison and punishment is an abomination which ought to be brought to an end" (59–60).

Although she does not develop her thoughts concerning terrorist acts in "Anarchism: What It Really Stands For," Goldman does defend certain terrorist acts as psychologically inevitable reactions of sensitive persons to the abuses of the state in her analysis of political violence elsewhere in *Anarchism and Other Essays*. Such sensitive individuals, seeing the misery and degradation of the masses and recognizing the state as the perpetrator of humankind's ills, are goaded by conscience and emotion into violent reprisals: "It is their supersensitiveness to the wrong and injustice surrounding them which compels them to pay the toll of our social crimes. . . . The burning, surging passion makes the storm inevitable." People like Leon Czolgosz, who assassinated President McKinley, are not lunatics or fanatics but are instead the most sensitive, idealistic individuals who merit compassion and admiration rather than condemnation. Although Goldman could not condone any violent acts because they violated the constructive spirit of anarchism, she could empathize with those driven to political violence.[28]

The only final answer to the abuses of the state, Goldman feels, is its abolition. To achieve individual growth and happiness, "government with its unjust, arbitrary, repressive measures must be done away with." She scorns those, including police, "flat heads," and "visionless dabblers in science," who insist on "the wickedness and weakness" of human nature as an impediment to the establishment of such a free environment. The current situation, Goldman asserts, thwarts human potential and distorts its image. Only anarchism can reveal the true essence of human nature and its possibilities (60–61).

Because she sees dynamism as the essence of anarchism, Goldman does not offer a single alternative. As "a living force in the affairs of our life," anarchism is "constantly creating new conditions." Anarchism, therefore, is not a dogmatic program to be carried out under any and all circumstances: "Methods must grow out of the economic needs of each place and clime, and of the intellectual and tempermental requirements of the individual. . . . Anarchy does not stand for military drill and uniformity; it does, however, stand for the spirit of revolt, in whatever form, against everything that hinders human growth" (63). As an individualistic anarchist, Goldman had an optimistic faith in the ability of human nature and intellect to meet challenges and create solutions. By the very tenets of her beliefs, however, she could have no single, simple blueprint for an anarchist future.

Although Goldman expressed her views more succinctly in another essay, "What I Believe," and developed aspects of her theory more fully in other writings, "Anarchism: What It Really Stands For" captures not only the essence of her philosophy but also the spirit of her rhetoric. The refutation of opponents' arguments, the caustic tone toward those who might disagree, and the colorful, if somewhat melodramatic language, are quintessentially Goldman. Alternating cogent reasoning with emotional hyperbole, she articulates a persuasive and entertaining defense of her opinions. To understand her anarchism fully, however, we must explore those essays that expand her critique of religion and explicate her defense of individualism.

"The Failure of Christianity" and "The Philosophy of Atheism"

With an atheism bordering on the obsessive, Goldman vehemently attacked all versions of religion. [29] Although this theme was common in her lectures, she published only two essays on it and did not include either in *Anarchism*. Her analysis and indictment of religion and her urging of atheism are significant, however, not only because they were central to her philosophy but also because they contributed to her persona and public notoriety.

Religion, Goldman asserts, dominates the human mind and originates from the combination of human insecurities and imagination: "As ignorance and fear are the parent of all superstition, the troubled fancy of primitive man wove the God idea." Although varying with the situations, religion always entails a dependence on God rather than on human potential and is, thus, antithetical to Goldman's belief in individualism. Even more distressing to her were the ways political leaders used religion. One of the more impressive covers from the May 1915 issue of *Mother Earth* conveys this view graphically: it shows popular evangelist Billy Sunday dancing with Christ, who had been taken down from the cross to accommodate the preacher's needs. She also contends that "consciously or unconsciously, most theists see in gods and devils, heaven and hell, reward and punishment, a whip to lash the people into obedience, meekness and contentment."[30] Religion constantly reinforces people's self-doubts and fears, while its insistence on divine omnipotence thwarts individual development, shackles human intellect, and enslaves humans.

The "slave mentality" that she saw as characteristic of the Christian religion was especially repugnant to her. By advocating docility in the face of adversity and by accepting the will of God, Christianity focuses attention on another world and makes people ignore the problems of this one, which they should be helping to correct. Following Nietzsche, she asserts that it is "most admirably adapted to the training of slaves, to the preparation of a slave society; in short, to the very conditions confronting us today. Indeed, never could society have degenerated to its present appalling state, if not for the assistance of Christianity." Christianity is a tool of the leaders because its teachings are a "more powerful protection against rebellion and discontent than the club or the gun."[31] Sharply attacking the Beatitudes, Goldman charges: "The reward in heaven is the perpetual bait, a bait that has caught man in an iron net, a strait jacket which does not let him expand or grow." Contrary to the instructive vitality of life, Christianity is, she concludes, "the conspiracy of ignorance against reason, of darkness against light, of submission and slavery against independence and freedom; of the denial of strength and beauty, against the affirmation of the joy and glory of life."[32] Entwined with the existing social and economic order, Christianity is, in its essence, antirevolutionary.

Her antidote to the spiritual poison of Christianity was atheism, which Goldman saw as a rising tide. Although individuals like Billy Sunday were using the "crudest and vulgarest" methods to lure people back to their churches and salvationist tents, theism was losing its appeal, she argues, as humans became "more engrossed in the problems of their immediate existence." Atheism, because it expresses "the expansion and growth of the human mind" and because its basis is in "an actual, real world with its liberating, expanding and beautifying possibilities," can emancipate mankind from all variations on the illusory God idea. "Mankind has been punished long and heavily for having created its gods. . . . Man must break his fetters which have chained him to the gates of heaven and hell, so that he can begin to fashion out of his reawakened and illumined consciousness a new world upon earth."[33]

"Minorities versus Majorities": The Individualist Anarchist

Despite her sympathy for the abused and oppressed masses, Goldman was too much of an individualist to share fully Kropotkin's belief that the inspiration for revolutionary leaders came from the people as a whole. Instead, she increasingly perceived the masses as impediments to social change. In "Minorities versus Majorities," her second essay in *Anarchism and Other Essays,* Goldman forcefully develops her analysis of the impact of the masses in society.

Labeling quantity as the spirit of the age that destroys quality, Goldman argues that this emphasis, "instead of adding to life's comforts and peace, has merely increased man's burden." The corruption that is evident in politics is the direct consequence of the blindness of the mass: "The majority cannot reason; it has no judgment. Lacking utterly in originality and moral courage, the majority has always placed its destiny in the hands of others. Incapable of standing responsibilities, it has followed its leaders even unto destruction."[34] As this passage implies, Goldman has no faith in the democratic process because majority rule not only infringes on the rights of the minorities but also reflects the limitations of the mass. The ballot produces not liberation for the people, but an allusion of power and the encouragement to limit the freedom of others to fit one's own prejudices. In a later passage she notes, "The most unpardonable sin in society is independence of thought. That this should be so terribly apparent in a country whose symbol is democracy, is very significant of the tremendous power of the majority" (73).

In answer to those who perceived the age as an era of individualism, Goldman insists that the opposite is the case. After pointing to the intolerance of educational innovation and the embracing of "the dietitians of predigested food *a la* Professors Eliot and Butler," she deplores the public taste in art as a "palate . . . like a dumping ground; it relishes anything that does not need mental mastication." The political rise of Theodore Roosevelt is further evidence that "public opinion is an omnipresent tyrant" and that "the majority represents a mass of cowards, willing to accept him who mirrors its own soul and mind poverty" (73–74).

Having proved it "absurd to claim that ours is the era of individualism," Goldman then insists that all progress emanates from the enlightened minority who are always "misunderstood, hounded, imprisoned, tortured, and killed." With a deft rhetorical flair, she educes the examples of Christ, Calvin, and Luther, all of whom were "like a sunrise amid the darkness of the night," before their ideas were appropriated and institutionalized by the mass. In American history, Goldman points to Thomas Jefferson, Patrick Henry, Thomas Paine, and various abolitionists as bold spirits who lead the way to truth. Finally, she mentions the rise of socialism as a lofty ideal that has been corrupted by public acceptance (76–77).

In her conclusion, she reaffirms her sympathy for the masses and their suffering. But she adds, "A compact mass . . . has never stood for justice and equality. It has suppressed the human voice, subdued the human spirit, chained the human body." Because of its nature, the majority has and can never produce innovation and growth. Such creative change can "become a reality only through the zeal, courage, the non-compromising determination of intelligent minorities, and not through the mass" (78).

Although "Minorities versus Majorities" contains Goldman's fullest explanation of her distrust of the masses, that theme echoes throughout her works. Frequently she reiterates her belief in the power of the liberated individual spirit and insists that concern for the individual's growth be primary. Indeed, her disappointment with the Russian Revolution stemmed in large part from its oppression and suppression of the individual.

The Russian Revolution: Anarchism and Reality

The Russian Revolution of 1917 initially promised to provide a pragmatic testing ground for Goldman's theories of human nature and social change. Her close identification with the Russian people and her faith in their spirit made her extraordinarily optimistic about the social changes promised by the Bolshevik leaders. Moreover, the leaders appeared to be committed to a kind of communism that paralleled her attitudes about economic organization and promised a healthy application of the theories she espoused. Her ultimate disillusionment is best understood against this backdrop of initial enthusiasm.

Having been sorely disappointed at the abortive Bolshevik uprising in 1905, Goldman applauds the spirit of the 1917 revolution
in the April issue of *Mother Earth,* hoping it "would prove strong
and vigorous enough to sweep beyond the boundaries of a merely
political reform movement. . . . The Russian people have set a
fine example to all other countries."[35] By December 1917 with the
ascendancy of Lenin, Trotsky, and Kollontay, she was confident of
the social revolution's success: "The new phase, the Bolysheviki
Revolution, lifts Russia out of the paralyzing position of a merely
political machine into a virile, active economic force."[36]

In pamphlets, speeches, and articles, she strongly endorses the
revolution, even rationalizing some questionable activities and
charging the American press with misrepresentation. She praises
Lenin and Trotsky for seeing beyond their own narrow theories and
for responding to "the compelling needs of the awakened Russian
people themselves. They have their ears close to the heartbeat of
the Russian people, who, while yet inarticulate, know how to register their demands much more powerfully through action."[37] The
Bolsheviks were, in her eyes, simply conduits of the people's will,
and their eagerness to serve in that capacity made them desirable
replacements for Kerensky's earlier, more rigidly doctrinaire regime.

Not only does Goldman defend the internal and external policies
of the Bolsheviks, but she cavalierly dismisses the opposition of
many traditional revolutionaries, like her theoretical mentor Peter
Kropotkin, to Bolshevik policies. "These good people have been
lured by the glamor of political liberalism . . . and have yet to
realize the line of demarcation between liberalism and autocracy is
purely imaginary." These objectors would, she felt, soon realize that
"the Bolysheviki represent the most fundamental, far-reaching and
all-embracing principle of human freedom and of economic well-
being."[38]

Reality proved a bitter teacher and Goldman completely altered
her views. After her two years of personal experience with Bolshevik
power in Russia, her compunction about her earlier unqualified
endorsement led her to write a seven-part series for the *New York
World* in 1922. In this series, she carefully distinguishes between
the ideals and spirit of the revolution, which she still supported,
and the forces presently in power, whom she repudiated. The revolution was, she felt, still viable despite its distortion and manip-
ulation by the Bolsheviks. In the series, Goldman also explicitly

castigates some policies of the Bolsheviks that she had earlier rationalized: the Brest-Litovsk Peace Treaty, centralization of production, forcible food collection, destruction of the Soviets, and the conscription of labor. She admiringly traces the trials of a longtime revolutionary heroine, Maria Spiridonova, under the Bolsheviks; and she at this time seconds Peter Kropotkin's compunctions about the revolution.[39] In sum, although the essays for the *New York World* reaffirm her commitment to the Russian Revolution, they completely repudiate her earlier support of the Bolsheviks. She illustrates and analyzes the deleterious impact of the Bolshevik regime on the Russian people and undertakes to refute the favorable press reports of its accomplishments, reports that she had earlier helped to write.

In *My Disillusionment in Russia* Goldman elaborates her explanations. Carefully tracing her experiences, she chronicles her gradual awakening to the unpleasant realities of revolutionary change under the Bolsheviks. In the afterword, however, she attempts to rescue her anarchist theories from the morass of Bolshevik *realpolitik*. First, Goldman is concerned to refute socialist charges that the revolution had failed because the country was not sufficiently industrialized. She offers evidence of the psychological readiness of the people for change, citing their fervent revolutionary sentiment and activities. "The people [were] carrying the Revolution into ever-widening channels."[40] Never a dogmatic dialectical materialist, Goldman argues that this psychological readiness is more significant than industrial development as a criterion for social revolution. Neither the Russian people nor Russia's stage of economic development is at fault; the Bolshevik leaders are.

The failure of the leaders stems from their insistence on retaining all the power of the traditional nation-state in the hands of the Communist party. Lenin was the real culprit, a man who "had very little concern in the Revolution" and to whom "Communism was a very remote thing." The centralized political state, Goldman insists, was "Lenin's deity, to which every thing else was to be sacrificed" (246). In Russia the Bolsheviks had substituted one form of state domination for another, while what was best in the revolution had "an entirely different object and in its very character . . . was the negation of authority and centralization." True communism, she insists, had never been tried in Russia. What occurred was "a libertarian step defeated by the Bolshevik State, by the temporary victory of the reactionary, the governmental ideal" (250–

51). Rather than being a failure of her anarchist theories, the Russian Revolution demonstrates beyond doubt that the state idea, which she had opposed in every guise, is "entirely and hopelessly bankrupt" (252).

Goldman summarizes her view: "The inherent tendency of the state is to concentrate, to narrow, and monopolize all social activities; the nature of the revolution is, on the contrary, to grow, to broaden, and disseminate itself in ever-wider circles. These two tendencies are incompatible and mutually destructive. The State idea killed the Russian Revolution" (257). Further, she concludes that the socialist conception of revolution is fundamentally wrong. Although the socialists argued that revolution is a "violent change of social conditions," Goldman, adopting the rhetoric of Nietzsche, insists that real revolution must entail "a fundamental transvaluation of values . . . not only of social but also human values." The Bolsheviks had attempted "to change only institutions and conditions while ignoring entirely the human and social values involved in the Revolution" (258–59).

Moreover, by using repressive methods employed in the old system and by arguing that the ends justified the means, the Bolsheviks had perverted the essence of revolution. Goldman contends that the means employed inevitably influenced the goal itself. Thus, the Bolsheviks' use of the old repressive techniques had not transformed Russian society nor allowed the revolution to be "the great *Teacher* of the *New Ethics.*" Their brutal methods had produced a "tragic condition" because "the means used to prepare the future become its cornerstone." In contrast, true revolution "is the mirror of the coming day; it is the child that is to be the Man of To-morrow" (261–63).

The immediate outcome of the Russian Revolution was a bitter disappointment to Goldman. Nevertheless, it convinced her more than ever of the evils of statism and the perils of using violence to achieve revolution. Although she retained her faith in the Russian spirit, she was also forced to acknowledge how easily revolutionary zeal could be misdirected and perverted. Her years in Russia also strengthened her commitment to individualism as the key element in anarchism, for she observed firsthand how actions undertaken in good faith for the general interest could insidiously repress and punish the most idealistic individuals, the very people who should be stimulating further revolutionary change. She concluded that the revolution failed because of flawed leadership and misdirection, rather than because of any inherent weakness in anarchist theories. The Bolshevik regime had not proven anarchist theory wrong but had betrayed anarchist theory in the interests of the consolidation of state power.[41]

Assessment of Goldman's Anarchism

In reading Goldman's philosophical and political essays, we are struck above all by her fervor and commitment. But her ideological sincerity does not obscure the weaknesses in her presentation of her ideas. Because she does not claim to be an innovative theorist, it is superfluous to charge her with a lack of originality. However, her role as a propagandist for social change required that her theories be both clear and practicable. Her indictments of the forces that hampered human development and created the dismal economic and social situation she perceived were direct and forceful. As she herself notes in her essay "Anarchism: What It Really Stands For," condemning an idea is less troublesome than attempting to understand it. In her own case, she was skillful at dissecting the problems of the extant system but far less adept at clarifying how to rectify them. Despite her long career as an activist and agitator, her thinking about anarchism contained several theoretical tensions that she never adequately resolved.

The clearest conflict in Goldman's thinking was that between the elitism implicit in her commitment to individualism and the egalitarianism intrinsic to anarchism. She argued convincingly at the Amsterdam conference in 1907 that collectives would only be effective if they were composed of strong individuals, but how such persons could be bound together, even if all were highly motivated, remained unclear. The very assertive individualism that she advocated could conceivably militate against the sacrificing of personal interest for group good. Her assertion that there was no necessary conflict between the two basic human urges, one toward society and the other toward individualism, is not self-evident; it rests on assumptions about human nature for which she offers no proof. Indeed, even her compelling analyses of contemporary society suggest that this view was overly optimistic. Her claims that human nature, unfettered by the constraints of the state, religion, and private property, would display the qualities essential for strong individuals to cooperate harmoniously are appealing but hardly convincing.

This tension between individualism and the requirements of the group produced another problem in her theories. Unlike Kropotkin, who felt the fervor for revolution lay buried in the masses, Goldman felt it must spring from the enlightened few. At the same time, she defended the validity of the 1917 Russian Revolution by arguing that the "psychology of the masses at a given period" was vital factor in meaningful social change.[42] Her attitude forced her into an elitism quite at odds with the egalitarian aspect of anarchism. Her skepticism about the mass and her insistence that it was never an innovative force made the mechanism for social change unclear. Were the elite few to stimulate change by stirring the benighted folk? If so, their approach would parallel that of the society they sought to change. Although Goldman touted the need for education to prepare the road for radical social changes, she presented an educational proposal that also smacked of propagandizing. In her strong insistence that acceptance by the mass and institutionalization corrupted even the noblest notions, she seemed to undercut the possibility of a society built on her own principles. In this respect, her theories are better as a model for the life of a rebel than as a foundation for a new society.

A second tension in her thinking appears in her analysis of how revolution could be accomplished. Once she relinquished her early support for violence as a tool, Goldman confronted the problem of how to initiate significant social and political change. This dilemma was complicated by her view that any social theory making a person "a conscious social unit, will act as a leaven for rebellion." Moreover, she realized that "resistance to tyranny is man's highest ideal. So long as tyranny exists, in whatever form, man's deepest aspiration must resist it as inevitably as man must breathe."[43] She also recognized that violence begot violence and that if it were accepted as an appropriate tool for revolution it would become counterrevolutionary, that is, it would reestablish the repressive values and policies the revolution sought to change.[44]

To resolve this dilemma, she offered two alternatives, both of which seem unrealistically optimistic. First, preparation before the revolution could minimize the necessity for violence. Goldman wrote to Havelock Ellis in 1925 that she had come to the conclusion "that the amount of violence in any revolution will depend entirely upon

the amount of preparation on the part of the conflicting forces—
the amount of *inner* preparation. By preparation I mean the growth
out of old habits and ideas."[45] Logically, she seems to say that the
preparation for revolution is the real revolution. Thus, ideally, if
"preparation" were adequate, there would be no need for eruptive
social change. This intellectual sleight of hand gets rid of the need
for violence, but it also makes sudden, significant, and deliberate
social and political change impossible.

Goldman's second hope was that anarchism would produce new
strategies for revolutionaries by stimulating their creative thinking.
Interestingly, Gandhi's techniques of nonviolent resistance did not
seem viable to her because they were not part of the Western cultural
heritage. His radical nonviolence was simply too great a departure
from the "old habits" to be of immediate use to revolutionaries in
the West. Goldman, however, concluded in a letter to Berkman in
1928 that "if we can undergo changes in every other method of
dealing with social issues, we will also learn to change in the methods
of revolution. I think it can be done. If not, I shall relinquish my
belief in revolution."[46] Despite her optimism, she was never able
to be more concrete than this in explaining how revolution was to
be brought about. The individualism that was so central to her
thinking prevented her from being willing to acquiesce to violence
as a means that sacrificed humans for the revolutionary cause.

Goldman's self-acknowledged problems in reconciling violence as
a necessary element in societal change with her reverence for individual life constitute a major weakness in her thought. Berkman
and others had less trouble because of their pragmatism and willingness to sacrifice the individual for the larger good. Goldman's
overriding focus on the individual made her unwilling to condone
violence, however. How her revolution was to be achieved without
breaking a few eggs remained unexplained in her public rhetoric.
She remained confused in her rhetorical stance that advocated radical
changes without explicating how they could be achieved. In her
correspondence during later years, she attempted to separate the
violence, which she had concluded was attendant on revolution,
from anarchism altogether. To one correspondent she wrote, "More
and more I come to the conclusion that there can be no Anarchist
Revolution. By its very violent nature Revolution denies everything
Anarchism stands for. The individual ceases to exist, all his rights
and liberties go under. In fact life itself becomes cheap and dehu-

manized." Several weeks later, Goldman depicted revolution as a natural force, comparable to climatological or geological upheaval, which must include violence by its very nature. In this context, "the function of Anarchism in a revolutionary period is to minimize the violence of the revolution and replace it by constructive efforts."[47] In essence, Goldman was forced to acknowledge that the theory she cherished was too avant-garde to be useful in correcting immediate problems.

These unresolved tensions in Goldman's thinking produce an apparent inconsistency in her published essays. Her prescription for the roles of the mass and the individual and her delineation of the mechanisms of social change remain elusive. As a result, the reader remains uncertain of key points in her philosophy. In drawing so eclectically from earlier thinkers and in devoting her energies to practical propaganda, Goldman never fully integrated her own thinking. Undoubtedly, critics and friends drew her attention to these problems.[48] Both her own forceful personality, which would daunt many questioners, and her idealistic and emotive view of an anarchistic future may have discouraged her careful consideration of these questions.

Aside from these unresolved tensions (or apparent inconsistencies), Goldman's theoretical essays also suffer from vagueness, emotionalism, and a kind of romanticism that is indistinguishable from wishful thinking. Despite her claims of clear-headedness and reasonableness, Goldman frequently fails to express her ideas clearly and to assess matters dispassionately. For example, the essays on syndicalism offer no definition of the term nor any explanation of how such worker cooperatives would function. In the same way, her claim that anarchism could free human beings does not reveal how such unfettering would occur. In part, this vagueness is a natural outgrowth of her anarchism, which insists on flexibility and individualism in solving problems. Consequently, to the uncommitted Goldman's explanations of anarchism, particularly of how it would operate, are vague and unconvincing. When the reader most needs the clarification of a concrete example or a specific description, Goldman lapses into the characteristic vagueness of Rousseauistic metaphors like "unchaining" human nature.

In both her vehement indictment of the three forces that thwarted the individual and in her rosy depiction of an anarchist future, Goldman employs an emotionalism that initially engages but ultimately detracts from the force of her essays. Her flagrantly loaded language and her sarcasm reduce some passages to harangues that seem at odds with her self-proclaimed role as a clear-headed, reasonable social critic and analyst. Moreover, her vitriol draws into question not only her fairness but her commitment to rational analysis of the issues involved. Conversely, in her descriptions of anarchism, she falls into a rhapsodic tone that again undermines her credibility as an objective analyst.

Goldman's strong emotional distaste for governments and for religion caused her to gloss over important differences and to overgeneralize at critical points. For example, she made no firm distinctions among forms of government, condemning democratic states and total dictatorships equally. This conflation obscured the fact that elected representatives were often more sensitive to public opinion and were forced into curtailing some abuses because of societal pressures. In the same way, her repugnance toward religion made her overlook the possibility that some religious groups and leaders could be forces for important social changes. Certainly, the civil rights movement of the 1960s would belie her wholesale indictment of religion. In essence, Goldman's emotional reactions on these topics overrode her commitment to reasoned analysis and sometimes reduced her rhetoric to diatribes against her pet enemies.

Despite her strong attacks on the mass, Goldman's assessment of human nature is highly idealistic. If human insecurities led individuals to create the state and religion, how can humankind be expected to sustain the freedom she envisions? We can hypothesize that Goldman might suggest that education can overcome this dilemma. Indeed, she suggests in one essay that human potential has been so stifled by repressive forces that we have no true picture of it. Still, the more skeptical reader can wonder if these forces do not control the darker as well as the brighter side of human nature. Her essays provide no clearcut resolution. There is no room in her philosophy for greed or the desire for power or jealousy. Her belief is that humankind, when freed from external constraints, will move into an individualistic Eden. She does not entertain the possibility that the competitiveness and self-interest she so frequently castigates as by-products of repressive social institutions are as integral to humans as the cooperativeness and compassion she prizes. Although she touts her objectivity and clear vision, Goldman's view of human nature seems reductively simplistic and naive. Again, she offers no systematic evidence or arguments for her analysis of human nature but simply presupposes it as a rhetorical axiom.

These flaws in Goldman's anarchism also suggest a source of its appeal. Goldman presents an optimistic vision that promises dignity and self-determination, especially to the downtrodden. Swept up by her undeniably powerful delivery, her audiences perhaps did not scrutinize her theories as carefully as her readers are able to do. Her picture of the better world-to-be is immediately powerful rhetorically, playing off of the hopes and aspirations of her listeners. Ironically, the rhetoric of Goldman's anarchism utilizes the same optimism and appeal to individualism that are claimed by the democratic capitalism she deplored; and her vision of an anarchist future borrows Edenic images from the theology she so abominated.

Chapter Three
Essays on Contemporary Issues

Clearing the soil from the rubbish of past and present.
—*Anarchism and Other Essays*

As a proponent of anarchism, Goldman was a stern social critic who analyzed contemporary issues and institutions from a firm ideological base. Although her ideology inevitably colored her perceptions and interpretations, it also frequently provided her with a fresh, incisive view on current topics, such as woman's rights and military preparedness. Central to Goldman's analysis of all issues was a concern for the autonomy of the individual and the desirability of nurturing personal growth. Whether she castigated the institution of marriage, the public schools, prisons, or militarism, her focus was always on how social pressures and institutions thwart individual development and victimize human beings. Her solution was, of course, a radical restructuring of society to destroy the political statism, capitalism, and puritanical morality which she saw as inimical to personal freedom.

Goldman's essays on social issues, largely rewritings of lectures presented earlier, typically appeared as articles in *Mother Earth* or as pamphlets published separately for sale or free distribution at meetings. In addition, in 1911 she published one collection, *Anarchism and Other Essays,* made up exclusively of essays on disparate social issues. In these diverse writings, four broad themes receive recurrent treatment: feminism, education, penology, and national chauvinism, which to Goldman included patriotism, military preparedness, and conscription.

Feminism

Goldman's focus on sexual issues distinguished her from many of her fellow anarchists. [1] Her own strong sexual nature, her difficulties

in achieving a balance between her personal longings and her independent commitment to anarchism, together with her experiences
working with women in sweat shops and nursing them in tenements,
made her keenly aware of the problems and dilemmas facing the
women of her day.[2] However, the root of Goldman's feminism lay
in the individualist foundation of her anarchism. Throughout her
writings, as she analyzed the social problems relating to women,
she stoutly maintained that the key to solving these difficulties lay
in women liberating themselves psychologically. "True liberation,"
she insisted, "begins in woman's soul."[3]

Anarchism and Other Essays includes four predominately feminist
works: "Marriage and Love," "Woman Suffrage," "The Traffic in
Women," and "The Tragedy of Woman's Emancipation." In addition, Goldman published "Victims of Morality," "The Woman
Suffrage Chameleon," and "The Social Aspects of Birth Control" in
Mother Earth. Throughout these essays, Goldman depicts women as
victims of social pressures that force them into stifling and dehumanizing roles. Surprisingly, she repudiates the suffrage and emancipation movements as a means of liberating women because she
feels that psychological freedom from society's mandates, not the
ballot nor any other "superficial" change, is the source of true
emancipation. Finally, she argues for the dissemination of birth
control information to allow women to control their bodies.

"Marriage and Love": The Crucial Difference

To understand Goldman's views on feminist topics, we must
begin with her concept of the ideal relationship between men and
women, for she thought that that union was crucial to personal
fulfillment for both sexes. In "Marriage and Love," she indicates
both the nature of the ideal relationship between the sexes and how
marriage impedes it. Her goal is a free, open relationship between
liberated men and women without taint of unnatural dependency,
a relationship sustained only by the bond of love. She envisions the
ideal relationship between the sexes at the end of the essay: "Some
day, some day, men and women will rise, they will reach the
mountain peak, they will meet big and strong and free, ready to
receive, to partake, and to bask in the golden rays of love."[4] This
free and equal relationship between individuals, furthering the po-
tentials of both without hindering the development of either, would

offer them the deepest fulfillment in life. For its creation and fruition, the independence and strength of both parties are essential. Unfortunately, to Goldman, societal forces at that time so constrained women that they were unable to become strong and self-reliant enough to participate in such an egalitarian relationship.

First of all, Goldman argues, economic and moral pressures encourage girls to pursue not love but marriage, a decadent institution that stifles natural impulses and ultimately enslaves them. Consequently, the ideal relationship that Goldman prized in theory seldom developed in practice, for the institution of marriage itself was culturally antagonistic to love. To Goldman marriage was primarily an economic arrangement, "an insurance pact," which a woman paid for "with her name, her privacy, her self respect, her very life." It was an arrangement that reduced her "to life-long dependency, to parasitism, to complete uselessness, individual as well as social." Since the pact also penalized man, primarily with "economic chains," Dante's warning over the entrance to the inferno, "Ye who enter here leave all hope behind," applied quite aptly to marriage. Fortunately, Goldman contends, the institution is crumbling because of its rotten foundations. As proof of the failure of the institution of marriage, Goldman points both to the rising divorce rate and to the many works of literature, like Ibsen's *A Doll's House,* that treat "the barrenness, the monotony, the sordidness, the inadequacy of marriage as a factor for harmony and understanding." Woman's gradual awakening to herself as "a being outside of the master's grace" was gradually undermining the institution of marriage. (228, 235).

To trace the fallacies underlying marriage and to expose how antagonistic it is to love, Goldman explores the alternatives open to women. If a woman seeks to enjoy sex without the sanction of marriage (as she insists any truly healthy woman would), she is "condemned as utterly unfit to become a wife of a 'good man,' his goodness consisting of an empty head and plenty of money." Thus, a shrewd woman must subdue her spirit, deny her nature, and stunt her vision simply to await a suitable marriage. This focus on marriage as woman's ultimate, exclusive goal prompted young girls in that "practical age" to think not of love but economic security: "Her dreams are not of moonlight and kisses, of laughter and tears; she dreams of shopping tours and bargain counters" (231–32).

Women's entrance into the work force had not altered their attitudes. Even when compelled by economic necessity to become wage earners, "who have the equal right with men to be exploited, to be robbed, to go on strike, aye to starve even," most women considered their positions as temporary preludes to the marriage they yearned for. This attitude, of course, made it difficult to entice them into labor unions, and they remained largely unsympathetic to labor agitation. Even working women who found a marriage partner were often compelled, unfortunately, to add the burdens of housework to their menial labor in shops and factories (233–34).

Ironically, the secure homes women sought were, to Goldman's eyes, an illusion. Marriage forced a woman to live in a sphere entirely controlled by her husband; she soon became nagging, "petty, quarrelsome, gossipy, unbearable, thus driving the man from the house." Such an environment offered a dismal home for children and degraded women by forcing them to become parasites. The protection the home allegedly provided for a woman was "in reality a snare, a travesty on human character" (234–35). The strongest indictment of marriage was the constraints it placed on motherhood, which Goldman characterizes as the "highest fulfillment of woman's nature." By denying women the right to bear children outside of marriage without social stigma and by compelling wives to conceive children in situations filled with hatred or under compulsion, the institution of marriage demonstrated the depth of its antagonism toward love (235–36).

The alternative to this deceptive, corrupt institution was free love. Labeling love "the strongest and deepest element in all life" and "the most powerful moulder of human destiny," Goldman argues that relationships based on it defy human constraints. Persons drawn together by love do not require the artificial "protection" of marriage, and children from such unions are assured of acceptance and security because they were conceived willingly by strong individuals bound only by their deep affection for each other. Although she acknowledges that "in our present pygmy state love is indeed a stranger to most people [because] its soul is too complex to adjust itself to the slimy woof of our social fabric," Goldman envisions a day when women and men would have the courage and "capacity to rise to love's summit" (237).

In contrasting her concept of the ideal relationship between men and women with the institution of marriage, this essay reflects many of Goldman's attitudes on issues related to women. While it concludes with a romantic vision of the new world possible when both sexes have freed themselves from the psychological constraints imposed by social conditioning, it does not probe the problems nor the implications created by such societal pressures. In other essays, Goldman not only examines the difficulties women faced as a result of social constraints, but she also exposes the fallacies and inadequacies of the proposed solutions. Her essays on prostitution, women's suffrage, puritanism, and the movement for woman's emancipation develop the themes she alludes to in her analysis of marriage and love.

The Plight of Women: Causes and Cures

To understand the plight of women from Goldman's perspective, we must first understand the forces working on them and the alternatives they faced. The three arch villains of anarchism—society, religion, and the state—operate to frustrate and thwart women in unique ways. Morality, condoned by organized religion and institutionalized in the lawmaking nation-state, pressured women to marry. By artificially regulating sexual behavior, the moral imperatives of these interlocking systems constricted a woman, Goldman argues, to three sexual alternatives: "the position of a celibate, a prostitute, or a reckless, incessant breeder of hapless children."[5] Each alternative has its horrors.

In "The Hypocrisy of Puritanism," Goldman exposes how that limited moral perspective penalizes women. The moral injunctions to female celibacy, growing out of puritanical attitudes, forced healthy men to seek out prostitutes and made otherwise healthy young women neurotic. Compelled to remain unnaturally celibate under pain of being considered immoral, young women suffered "neurasthenia, impotence, depression, and a great variety of nervous complaints involving diminished power of work, limited enjoyment of life, sleeplessness, and preoccupation with sexual desires and imaginings." Citing the reasoning of Freud, Goldman even contends that this repression probably explained the "mental inequality of the sexes": women's "intellectual inferiority . . . is due to the inhibition of thought imposed upon them for the purpose of sexual repression."[6]

Marriage, the only arena for sexual activity condoned by Puritanism, produces different but equally horrendous results. First, it encourages jealousy and possessiveness, qualities that are antithetical to the individual freedom Goldman prizes. Besides undermining a woman's independence and warping her character and personality, as Goldman explained in her essay on marriage and love, puritanical morality operating within the institution of marriage also compels a woman into motherhood. The consequences of such forced child-bearing are not only physically and emotionally draining for the woman, but also cause her to risk her life in abortions and deprive her children of proper care. The same Puritanism which forces un-natural continence on the unmarried girl "blesses her married sister for incontinent fruitfulness in wedlock." Denied access to safe meth-ods of birth control, the very mention of which was considered criminal, women are forced to bear children "irrespective of weak-ened physical condition or economic inability to rear a large fam-ily. . . . Thanks to this Puritan tyranny, the majority of women soon find themselves at the ebb of their physical resources. Ill and worn, they are utterly unable to give their children even elementary care. That, added to economic pressure, forces women to risk utmost danger rather than continue to bring forth life." Noting that "the custom of procuring abortions in America has reached such vast proportions as to be almost beyond belief," Goldman refers to sta-tistics that indicated that seventeen abortions were committed for every one hundred pregnancies. Although this "fearful percentage" represented only the cases known to physicians, it helped prove that "Puritanism continuously exacts thousands of victims to its stupidity and hypocrisy."[7]

Finally, she stresses, a woman who follows her natural and healthy sexual desires outside marriage faces a wretched fate indeed. Because society insists on purity for women and because it prides itself on keeping them sexually ignorant, the woman who explores her sex-uality without the "protection" of marriage experiences guilt, re-morse, and degradation. Overwhelmed by a sense of her own wickedness, she is easily drawn into the "maelstrom" of prostitution. The causes of this malign institution in the social and economic system in which Goldman lived are the focus of "The Traffic in Women," included in *Anarchism and Other Essays*.

In writing the essay, Goldman was responding to the outcries of outraged reformers who had "suddenly made a great discovery—the white slave traffic." Their recent concern and the publicity that turned woman's tragedy into "a toy with bright colors" to attract society's attention irked her. She felt the reformers were zealots, "indifferent to the sufferings and distress of the victims of prostitution" and to the economic abuses that promoted it.[8]

In regulating sexual activity artificially and in thwarting healthy drives, puritanical morality contributed to the development of prostitution; but factors other than morality encouraged women to become prostitutes. An economic system that offered too little pay for labor, especially for woman's labor, also forced women onto the streets. In commenting on the recent alarm over the "traffic in women," Goldman finds the roots of the problem in capitalistic abuses:

> What is the real cause of the trade in women? Not merely white women but yellow and black women as well. Exploitation, of course; the merciless Moloch of capitalism that fattens on underpaid labor, thus driving thousands of women and girls into prostitution. With Mrs. Warren [of Shaw's play] these girls feel, "Why waste your life working for a few shillings a week in a scullery, eighteen hours a day?" Naturally, our reformers say nothing about this cause. They know it well enough but it doesn't pay to say anything about it. It is much more profitable to play the Pharisee, to pretend an outraged morality, than to go to the bottom of things (178).

To substantiate the link between capitalistic exploitation and prostitution, Goldman turns to statistics and expert opinion. For example, she notes that the average yearly wage of women factory workers is $280, a clearly inadequate income. She cites a contemporary study of the history of prostitution that had also concluded that it was a direct result of such inadequate pay. The same study had determined by a survey of 2,000 prostitutes that only a few came from comfortable, middle-class homes. The majority were working-class women, "some driven into prostitution through sheer want, others because of a cruel, wretched life at home" (179–80).

Having established the economic basis for the problem, Goldman traces the psychological processes that moved young women into such a demeaning way of life. Faced with the prospect of long hours in crowded conditions for little pay and lacking even a comfortable home as a refuge after work, young girls saw "the street or some place of cheap amusement" as a "means of forgetting their daily routine." Contact with the opposite sex in such places, coupled with the girl's "over-sexed" state, produced the natural, predictable response. The consequences of sexual experimentation for the young

woman, while equally predictable given society's false morality, were
often tragic. Although it was a "conceded fact" that a woman was
raised as a "sex commodity," Goldman insists that she was nonetheless "kept in absolute ignorance of the meaning and importance
of sex" (184). Moreover, society's double standard of sexual morality
put a girl at a tremendous disadvantage:

Society considers the sex experiences of a man as attributes of his general
development, while similar experiences in the life of a woman are looked
upon as a terrible calamity, a loss of honor and of all that is good and
noble in the human being. This double standard involves keeping the
young in absolute ignorance on sex matters, which together with an
overwrought and stifled sex nature, helps to bring about a state of affairs
that our Puritans are so anxious to avoid or prevent (185–86).

Having had her first sexual experience outside marriage, the girl
inevitably feels herself "depraved and fallen . . . a complete outcast,
with the doors of home and society closed in her face." Since "the
meanest, most depraved and decrepit man still considers himself
too good to take to wife the woman whose grace he was quite willing
to buy," the young woman is forced into the life of a prostitute,
where she is further debased and hounded by the very social forces
that had engineered her fall. Goldman bitterly castigates the mor-
alists who condemn prostitutes, for such women, she emphasizes,
like prisoners, are the victims of society (187).

Goldman believed that the movement to free women from the
confines of marriage and to open new vistas had created different
but still substantial problems. In "The Tragedy of Woman's Emancipation," Goldman explores the dilemmas that this effort had produced. Achieving harmony between the sexes did not, in her view,
mandate a "superficial equalization of human beings." Rather, it
required understanding and appreciating their differences and their
separate virtues. A woman who sought emancipation, who eschewed
marriage and avoided prostitution, faced the problem of "how to
be one's self and yet in oneness with others, to feel deeply with all
human beings and still retain one's own characteristic qualities."
The goal of emancipation should be to allow one to develop all sides
of one's nature and to revel in one's individuality: "Emancipation
should make it possible for woman to be human in the truest sense.
Everything within her that craves assertion and activity should reach

its fullest expression; all artificial barriers should be broken, and the road towards greater freedom cleared of every trace of centuries of submission and slavery."[9]

Unfortunately, the woman's emancipation movement had "isolated" woman and "robbed her of the fountain springs of that happiness which is so essential to her." Since reformers had succeeded in removing some external fetters without changing the fundamental moral strictures of religion, law, and social code, a liberated woman became the most unnatural type: a sexless, loveless creature competing with men instead of cooperating with them. The liberated woman might be economically independent but she was condemned to emotional death. "Merely external emancipation has made of the modern woman an artificial being, who reminds one of the products of French arboriculture with its arabesque trees and shrubs, pyramids, wheels, and wreaths; anything except the forms which would be reached by the expression of her own inner qualities. Such artificially grown plants of the female sex are to be found in large numbers, especially in the so-called intellectual sphere of our life." Paradoxically, the woman who wished to be truly free, Goldman avers, must begin by "emancipating herself from emancipation."[10]

The problem with emancipation, as it was practiced, stemmed from its focus on economic independence and equality. Moved into the workplace on equal footing with men, women lacked the physical resources to compete with them. As a consequence, many either exhausted themselves in a futile attempt to match the performance of men or, realizing the costs of that effort, escaped from such "independence" into the "security of marriage." Moreover, the emphasis on independence caused women to stifle their instincts and to deny their natural impulse toward love and motherhood. Professional women, in particular, struggled to maintain a "dignified, proper appearance, while the inner life is growing empty and dead." Their tragedy lay not in having too many life-enhancing experiences but in having too few. To such "intellectual" women, emancipation from traditional sex roles too often meant a denial of their essential, precious sexuality, Goldman believed. Viewing men and family life as impediments to her career, such a woman became a "mere professional automaton . . . because of the chains of moral and social prejudice that cramp and bind her nature." In essence, Goldman claims "the movement for woman's rights has broken many old fetters, but it has also forged new ones."[11]

In biting essays on woman's suffrage, Goldman repudiates that movement as well. First, because she was skeptical of any representative form of government and abhorred any man-made laws that infringed on the freedom of other individuals, she argues that suffrage merely deluded the masses into submitting to the state; thus voters within a fundamentally unjust system were adding their voluntary complicity to the repressions enforced by the state. Second, destroying individual dignity, suffrage corrupted people by inviting them to make laws with which to control others. Furthermore, Goldman repeatedly stresses that evidence indicated that woman's suffrage did not produce meaningful social change for women or other workers. Finally, she argues that giving women the vote had substantial hazards because in society's present debased state women are unlikely to make wise political choices but instead can be expected to augment the status quo. "Woman's narrow and purist attitude toward life," Goldman avers, "makes her a greater danger to liberty wherever she has political power. . . . Her life-long parasitism has utterly blurred her conception of the meaning of equality. . . . In her exalted conceit, she does not see how truly enslaved she is, not so much by man, as by her own silly notions and traditions. Suffrage cannot ameliorate that sad fact; it can only accentuate it."[12]

The whole women's emancipation movement was failing, Goldman felt, because it concentrated on external factors that, while important, were not the crux of the problem. Emancipating women from arbitrary external constraints, like giving them the right to vote, was senseless if individual women did not first liberate themselves internally from unconscious enslavement to the reigning religious, political, and social prejudices. "True emancipation begins neither at the polls nor in courts. It begins in woman's soul. . . . It is, therefore, far more important for her to begin with inner regeneration, to cut loose from the weight of prejudices, traditions, and customs." By freeing themselves from such traditional strictures and by realizing that harmony between the sexes is essential to their happiness, women can prepare themselves to experience the delights of real communion between men and women. Only that, Goldman opines, can "fill the emptiness and transform the tragedy of woman's emancipation into joy, limitless joy."[13]

Although Goldman's vision of the possible future relationship between the sexes was idealistic and romantic, she perceived important practical problems that required immediate attention before such a utopian world could exist. As her views on motherhood and childbearing suggest, support for birth control was an essential aspect of her feminism and an important adjunct to her anarchism. Goldman perceptively recognized that until women could control their bodies by protecting themselves from unwanted pregnancies they would be forced to exhaust their physical and mental energies in producing children who would further drain and diminish their resources. Although she continued to insist that psychological liberation was the keystone of women's emancipation, she also knew that until women could control their reproductive role they could not exercise the freedom she envisioned for them.

By her own record, Goldman lectured on birth control long before her arrest in March 1916. Following Margaret Sanger's arrest for the publication of *The Woman Rebel,* Goldman became more explicit in her own talks. [14] Her arrest and subsequent trial for discussing contraceptives led her to publish "The Social Aspects of Birth Control" as an essay in *Mother Earth,* her only written statement on the topic. In the essay, she attempts to outline the contemporary factors that heralded a changing attitude toward contraception.

To begin her discussion, she depicts birth control as a "great idea," which like all innovations, is only slowly being accepted by society. While this delay is "only one more proof of the sluggishness of the human mind," her usual villains, the state in the form of militarism and exploitative capitalism, are deeply involved in the resistance. Drawing on the arguments of Thomas Malthus, "the father of birth control," she insists that capitalism, which used up the masses in its factories, and militarism, which used them for cannon fodder, both were "in favor of a large and excessive race and are therefore opposed to Birth Control." The capitalists, dependent on a large mass of unemployed, which the dismal science of economics designated "the labor margin," desired "that under no circumstances must the labor margin diminish, else the sacred institution known as capitalistic civilization will be undermined." Goldman observed factors in society, including the awakening of women and the increasing awareness of overpopulation as a problem, that mandated widespread education and gave her hope about birth control. [15]

Having outlined the forces that were prompting a changed attitude toward contraception, Goldman attacks those who oppose the movement in the name of motherhood and who castigate women supporting the movement as irresponsible and even immoral. It is, she contends, woman's keen sense of responsibility for the race and her desire for a better world that stimulated her interest in birth control. "Never before has she been able to see in the child, not only in her child, but every child, the unit of society, the channel through which man and woman must pass; the strongest factor in the building of a new world."[16]

If statutes on the books impede this movement, then they must go. "After all, that is what laws are for, to be made and unmade. How dare they demand that life shall submit to them?" Her role in the process is to challenge the laws by discussing the topic openly. Her commitment to birth control makes her contemptuous of the consequences. "I stand as one of the sponsors of a worldwide movement," she prophesies, "to set women free from this terrible yoke and bondage of enforced pregnancy; a movement which demands the right of every child to be well born; a movement which shall help free labor from its eternal dependence. . . . I may be arrested, I may be tried and thrown into jail, never will I be silent; never will I acquiesce . . . nor will I make peace with a system which degrades woman to a mere incubator and which fattens on her innocent victims."[17]

While Goldman's views on these issues presage many of the arguments and attitudes of the modern woman's movement, she did not identify herself with contemporary feminists. Indeed, as we have seen, she was critical both of the suffrage movement and of most women who saw themselves as emancipated. Her feminism was inextricably embedded in her individualistic anarchism and reflected her concern for broader social issues. For example, when the leaders of the suffrage movement endorsed the United States' involvement in World War I, Goldman castigated them for their shortsightedness and argued that their support for the war refuted their claims that enfranchised women would be a constructive force in society.[18] As she wrote to her niece, "I flatter myself to have been more interested in the fate of woman and by far from a broader and deeper point of view than those who label themselves Feminists and have no interest whatever in the general social question."[19] Not only did Goldman differ from many of her contemporaries in setting the "woman's question" in a larger social framework, but she also perceived the need for painful psychological change as the primary phase of liberation. If liberation had to begin in woman's soul, a woman must be willing to pay the price of growth and development "or remain in the dull state of the cow. For it is not only the modern woman, but all civilized people who pay a certain price for their awakening."[20] These differences in emphasis make Goldman's feminism particularly appealing to some who are active in the current women's movement.

If Goldman's attitudes distinguish her from others working for feminist causes at the same time, they also differentiate her from fellow anarchists. Her insistence on the significance of issues related to women and on the importance of sexuality in human life were hallmarks of her interpretation of anarchism. Her extensive treatment of these themes in her speaking and writing not only distinguished her from other agitators, but it also contributed to her notoriety. Altogether her often perceptive attitudes on feminist issues provide an interesting, concrete application of her anarchist ideology.

Education

Goldman's commitment to nonviolent social change and her concern for nurturing individualism drew her attention to contemporary education, which she criticized, as might be expected, for stifling children's natural development. She offered her analysis in three published essays which directly address educational issues: "The Child and Its Enemies," "Francisco Ferrer and the Modern School," and "La Ruche." A fourth essay that exists in typescript, "The Social Importance of the Modern School," probably constitutes notes for her lecture on the subject. In these works, Goldman criticizes society's handling of children in the home and in the schools while she extols the modern school movement as a healthy, hopeful alternative to contemporary educational practices.

"The Child and Its Enemies."   This essay, which appeared in the second issue of *Mother Earth,* provides a sharp critique of the treatment and education of children. Goldman begins by posing what she sees as the key issue in the form of a very loaded question: "Is the child to be considered as an individuality, or as an object to be moulded according to the whims and fancies of those about it? . . . whether the child is to grow within, whether all that craves expression will be permitted to come forth toward the light of day;

or whether it is to be kneaded like dough through external forces."
Since humankind is best served by strong individuals and since the
child is the father of the adult, the child must be encouraged to
grow and develop naturally into a strong-minded individual. But
because all institutional forces perceive the strong individual as a
threat, Goldman believes that "every effort is being made to cramp
human emotion and originality of thought in the individual into a
straight-jacket from its earliest infancy; or to shape every human
being according to one pattern; not into a well-rounded individual,
but into a patient work slave, professional automaton, tax-paying
citizen, or righteous moralist."[21]

Both parents and schools stifle the natural development of children, Goldman argues. At an early age a child who shows "individual
tendencies in its play" receives "everlasting external interference in
its world of thought and emotion." Even parents whose beliefs differ
radically from the social consensus mold their children according to
their lights of right and wrong, merely substituting their radical
views for more conventional propaganda. Since the obstacles placed
in the way of individual growth are so numerous, it is "a miracle"
if a child retains its strength and beauty and survives "the various
attempts at crippling that which is most essential to it."[22]

The educational system is even worse, as Goldman draws the lurid
contrast, because its ideal is not "complete, well-rounded, original
being[s]" but rather "automatons of flesh and blood, to best fit into
the treadmill of society and the emptiness and dullness of our lives."
Drumming dead facts into a child's brain, teachers handicap the
child in gaining "a true understanding of the human soul and its
place in the world." Instead, these dead facts serve "to maintain
every form of authority and to create much awe for the importance
of possession." Like Dickens's Gradgrind in *Hard Times,* "Instructors
and teachers, with dead souls, operate with dead values." Such
instruction has direct political consequences by producing "dull,
shallow patriotism, blind to its own limitations, with bull-like
stubbornness, utterly incapable of judging the capacities of other
nations." Furthermore, these instructors make history "a cheap pup-
pet show, where a few wire-pullers are supposed to have directed
the course of development of the entire human race." Because such
miseducation deadens the intellect, Goldman advises that "predigested food" should be inscribed over every school "as a warning to

all who do not wish to lose their own personalities and their original sense of judgment."[23]

If the child is intellectually stifled, he or she confronts equally great obstacles in emotional development. Bombarded by imperatives—"You shall! You must! This is right! That is wrong!"—the child has to battle against both internal and external force. A young child subjected to such pressures resembles "a young delicate tree that is being clipped and cut by the gardener in order to give it an artificial form." Such a young person will, Goldman warns, "never reach the majestic height and the beauty it would if allowed to grow in nature and freedom." Moreover, social morality, strongly reinforced in the schools, perverts normal sexuality so that "the love and tender feelings in the young plant are turned into vulgarity and coarseness through the stupidity of those surrounding it." The only hope for the future lies in guaranteeing the free growth and development of children so that they can create a "free community which shall make interference and coercion of human growth impossible."[24]

In her lecture notes for an unpublished essay on "The Social Importance of the Modern School," Goldman develops her indictment against traditional educational practices and explains the approach of the modern school movement. Answering the question she has raised about the nature of the traditional school, she responds with a characteristically hyperbolic metaphor: "It is for the child what the prison is for the convict and the barracks for the soldier— a place where everything is being used to break the will of the child, and then to pound, knead, and shape it into a being utterly foreign to itself." The systematic drilling used in schools resembles compulsory feeding and is equally abhorrent. The greatest harm of this approach is not that it teachs nothing worth knowing nor that it perpetuates the class structure; rather its greatest injury stems from its "boastful proclamation that it stands for true education," a claim that deludes and further enslaves the masses.[25]

In contrast, the school Goldman advocates begins with a sounder assumption and produces a superior result. The modern school repudiates the "pernicious and truly criminal system of education" and rejects compulsion as the antithesis of education. "The underlying principle of the Modern School is this: education is a process of drawing out, not of driving in; it aims at the possibility that the child should be left free to develop spontaneously, directing his own efforts and choosing the branches of knowledge which he desires to study." In this libertarian environment, the teacher, a guide or "channel" for the children's explorations, should inspire the child without external discipline. The Rousseauistic goal is to enable the child "to know himself, to know his relation to his fellowmen, and to realize himself in a harmonious blending with society." She envisions the dawning of a new day "when the school will serve life in all phases and will reverently lift each human child to its appropriate place in a common life of beneficent social efficiency, whose motto will be not uniformity and discipline but freedom, expansion, good will, and joy for each and all."[26]

In her essays on the experimental schools of Francisco Ferrer in Spain and Sebastian Faure in France, Goldman traces the development of the modern school abroad and outlines its approaches. A visit to La Ruche, Faure's school outside Paris, convinced her that he was "a practical idealist—one that applies his theories of a happier future to the immediate regeneration of society." She was especially impressed with the physical attractiveness of Faure's school, with the children's demeanor, and with his egalitarianism. He noted that his children, drawn from the least privileged classes, showed a remarkable "love of study, the desire to know, to be informed. They have learned a new method of work—one that quickens the memory and stimulates the imagination."[27] Faure's approach was, for Goldman, the key to peaceful but radical social change, although her essays do not provide a full description of his methods.

Her essay on Francisco Ferrer describes his efforts to develop a school in Spain modeled on Faure's and offers a brief history of the modern school movement in France. In a broader sense, however, the essay is a eulogy for Ferrer, who had been executed for his alleged participation in a political uprising. Goldman traces his political problems to his innovative school, which undermined the Catholic Church's control of education in Spain. Ferrer's death was not in vain, she insists, because his martyrdom has inspired people throughout the world to develop schools based on his model.[28]

In her discussions of education and in her advocacy for alternative schools, Goldman was characteristically perceptive and vague. Her indictments of dehumanizing educational methods and her emphasis on the importance of encouraging each child to develop naturally became clarions for later educational reformers. Although her attitudes were closely tied to her ideology, many of her criticisms were intelligent and accurate. As was frequently true of Goldman's writing and speaking, however, she was better at diagnosing problems than at offering solutions. Consequently, her discussions of education are stimulating but simultaneously frustrating and unsatisfying. We are convinced by her analysis, but uncertain about how to implement reforms that can correct the problems.

Crime and Punishment: "Prisons: A Social Crime and Failure"

Emma Goldman's concern for the oppression of the individual by society and her libertarian views made her alert to flaws in the penal system. Because she felt that the state, capitalism, and religion thwarted healthy individual growth, Goldman perceived prisoners as victims of society rather than as guilty perpetrators of crime against their fellow men. [29] She reprehended the rationale for the very existence of prisons as well as criticized specific penal practices, while consistently expressing compassion for the inmates. If she idealized prisoners and offered simplistic analyses of criminal behavior, her essay "Prisons: A Social Crime and Failure," included in *Anarchism and Other Essays,* nevertheless provides a well-organized, clear-headed indictment of the weaknesses of contemporary penology.

Using a parable from Dostoyevsky to demonstrate that prisons were hells on earth, she notes that, in contradiction of the boasts of social reformers, "human beings continue to be sent to the worst of hells, wherein they are outraged, degraded, and tortured, that society might be 'protected' from phantoms of its own making." [30] Oscar Wilde's assessment of prisons as the breeding ground for "vilest deeds" and the destruction of all that is good in humans accorded with her perception of their impact on society. Moreover, the expenditure of huge sums to keep persons "caged up like wild beasts" had not reduced the crime rate; indeed it had soared. To explain why prisons had failed so dramatically, Goldman examines the nature and causes of crime and society's methods of coping with it in her essay.

Using Havelock Ellis's classification of the four types of crimes—the political, the passional, the insane, and the occasional—Goldman states that political and passional crimes are due to good individuals driven to violence by circumstances. The insane criminal is also not fully responsible for his or her deeds. These three classes, therefore, do not require rehabilitation and do not deserve the terrible punishment of incarceration. The occasional group are victims of society, for they are "conditioned in our cruel social and economic arrangement" and "a thorough investigation would prove that nine crimes out of ten could be traced, directly or indirectly, to our economic and social iniquities, to our system of remorseless exploitation and robbery." Labeling economic, political, moral, and physical factors the "microbes of crime," she moves her attention to how the society in which she lived coped with the problem.[31]

The four methods that society has used to handle crime—revenge, punishment, deterrence through fear, and reform—have all failed miserably. Punishment has proved ineffective because it assumes that humans are free to choose, rather than compelled into actions by the social and economic situation. Likewise, attempts at deterrence through fear of punishment are useless because they degrade and debase humans to the extent that they are left powerless and unable to cope with life at all. The most common of these alternatives, society's punitive measures, administered under brutal conditions in prisons, do not rehabilitate such criminals but dehumanize and degrade them, producing "an emaciated, deformed, will-less, ship-wrecked crew of humanity, with the Cain mark on their foreheads, their hopes crushed, all natural inclinations thwarted."[32]

To improve the situation Goldman suggests several measures. First, she urges an increase in social awareness of the "rudiments of crime in us." Such understanding, she feels, will make humankind more empathetic with the criminal and eager to improve the treatment. Within prisons, she insists, inmates must have the opportunity for meaningful work at reasonable pay to develop their skills for use outside. She urges unions to support such employment at reasonable wages to prevent future economic frustrations for released criminals, to protect their own wages, and to lessen the possibility that released prisoners will be drawn into employment as "scales, black-legs, detectives and policemen." Finally, Goldman sees the need for commutable sentences to provide hope and incentive for the rehabilitated prisoner. Although these specific reforms might temporarily ameliorate the situation, she concedes that the only long-term hope lies in an anarchist restructuring of society that would eliminate the economic and political roots of crime. "Nothing short of a complete reconstruction of society will deliver mankind from the cancer of crime."[33]

National Chauvinism: Patriotism, Preparedness, Militarism, and Conscription

Although Goldman attacked patriotism as early as 1908, her objections to it grew more salient and intense with the beginning of World War I. Not only did she feel that patriotism was a misguided emotion, but she saw its direct relationship to militarism, which she deplored. Because she saw militarism as exploiting workers and enriching capitalists while obscuring the real foes of all workers, she vehemently opposed military preparedness and, later, conscription.

In her essay "Patriotism: A Menace to Liberty," included in *Anarchism and Other Essays,* Goldman develops her objections to the concept of patriotism quite persuasively. Admitting that nostalgia for the land of one's youth is a legitimate emotion, she contrasts that feeling with the false patriotism encouraged by unscrupulous politicians and warmongers. Quoting Samuel Johnson, she avers that "patriotism is the last resort of scoundrels" and that it serves to justify wholesale murder. In reality, she argues, patriotism is a superstition "artificially created and maintained through a network of lies and falsehoods," and she lists conceit, arrogance, and egotism as its essentials. Despite its emotional appeal, based on artificial geographic boundaries and feelings of superiority stemming from these divisions, patriotism compels men to kill one another in attempts to impose their supposed superiority on others. Moreover, this false pride and emotional furor stimulate the development of costly armies and navies to defend territory, which further burdens the workers and exhausts resources that should go to more positive, live-enhancing uses. Citing the vast military expenditures and computing the costs to each citizen, Goldman concludes that the increasing demands of such militarism threaten each nation with "a progressive exhaustion both of men and resources."[34]

In addition to these costs, patriotism also demands blind allegiance to a flag and a willingness to die in what are essentially economically motivated confrontations. As an example, Goldman cites the Spanish-American War, which was fought "in consideration of the price of sugar." In truth, "the lives, blood, and money of the American people were used to protect the interests of American capitalists, which were threatened by the Spanish government." The capitalists, who profited from militarism and war and who had for

centuries enslaved the masses, understood mass psychology and used
armies and navies as "the people's toys" to distract them from the
"despair, sorrow and tears" that grew out of their economic
exploitation.[35]

The saddest victim of patriotism, however, is the soldier, "that
poor, deluded, victim of superstition and ignorance. . . . What
has patriotism in store for him? A life of slavish submission, vice,
and perversion, during peace; a life of danger, exposure, and death,
during war." Objecting to the perpetuation of the class system
within ranks—soldiers wasting "their young days, polishing the
boots and brass buttons of their superior officers"—she adds, "The
growth of the standing army inevitably adds to the spread of sex
perversion; the barracks are the incubators." By giving men "habits
of idleness and a taste for excitement and adventure," the army
unfits men for civilian life.[36] The result is that the soldier becomes
an automaton, without dignity or integrity.

In her eyes, militarism was a natural extension of patriotic fervor
and both were the underpinnings of capitalism. She saw hope,
however, in the growing realization of "thinking men and women
the world over" that "patriotism is too narrow and limited a conception to meet the necessities of our time."[37]

With the outbreak of war in Europe, Goldman repeatedly spoke
against demands for American preparedness, warning in a strained
metaphor of "the deadly grip of the war anesthesis . . . the mad
teeming fumes of a blood soaked chloroform, which has obscured
its [mankind's] vision and paralyzed its heart."[38] She urged her audiences to oppose the special interest groups "which consciously and
deliberately work for the increase of armament, whose purposes are
furthered by creating the war hysteria." Her targets included armament and munitions manufacturers, "the jingo howls of the press,
the blood and thunder tirades of bully Roosevelt, the sentimental
twaddle of our college-bred President." Further, she argued that
militarism led to war and used up valuable resources: "Militarism
consumes the strongest and most productive elements of each nation.
Militarism swallows the largest part of the national revenue. Almost
nothing is spent on education, art, literature and science compared
with . . . militarism in times of peace, while in times of war
everything else is set at naught, all life stagnates, all effort is curtailed." The real war, she insisted, should be between classes and
against "false values, against evil institutions, against all social

atrocities."[39] Having argued that the prejudices underlying the war were antithetical to America's cosmopolitan blending of ethnic groups and that European politics should be of no concern in this country, Goldman emphasized the disastrous impact of the war mania on the nation: the threat of compulsory military training, the further enrichment of capitalists, the increased persecution of workers, and the suppression of dissenters.[40]

Frustrated in her attempts to solidify workers against the war, Goldman decries the lack of provisions for conscientious objectors in "The No-Conscription League," a brief essay, and points out that "the 'land of the free and the home of the brave' is ready to coerce free men into military yoke." Setting out the principles of the No-Conscription League she had founded, Goldman vows, that members "not unmindful of the difficulties in our way" are resolved to spare "no effort to make the voice of protest a moral force in the life of this country."[41] She offers a particularly melodramatic depiction of what she perceived America's reaction would be when conscription took effect on 5 June 1917: "The Moloch Militarism will sit in pompous state awaiting its victims who are to be dedicated to its gluttonous appetite. . . . Music will drown the groans and curses of the unwilling." In contrast to Europe, where such occasions had been accompanied by general grief and unhappiness, "human tragedy has ever been the cause of rejoicing" in America, "a holiday participated in by a joy-drunk mob gloating over the agony of its victims . . . while the Moloch Militarism sets on his bloody throne ready to devour the sacrifice, yet proclaiming in loud dissonant tones: Praise unto Democracy! Glory unto War!"[42]

Conclusion

The impact of Goldman's anarchism on her discussion of social issues is particularly clear in her analyses of the causes of problems. The roots of each difficulty are unwarranted societal constraints and pressures on the individual. This ideological bias sometimes obscured her vision and limited her perspective. For example, her classification of types of crime, while it fits her ideology, conflates many disparate acts under the rubrics of "passional" and "occasional." Moreover, she too readily assumes that society alone is responsible for passional and political crimes. Her attacks on woman's suffrage overlook the symbolic importance of that measure, and her analyses of women's choices present only the bleak side of each alternative. Although Goldman's observations contain some truth, significant distortions are also apparent. Like a wide-angle lens on a camera, her anarchism widens her field but distorts her vision. Still, despite her bias, many of her arguments were and remain cogent and insightful. The significance of birth control for women and the necessity of psychological liberation, which she perceived, are key issues for the modern feminist movement. Her views on the impact of defense spending also accord with the observations of many modern critics. Moreover, many of her suggestions about prison reform have become common practices. Goldman was often in advance of her age in seeing and understanding problems. Irritatingly simplistic as many found her panaceas, her lectures and essays undoubtedly stimulated and challenged her contemporaries. A review of *Anarchism and Other Essays* in the *Los Angeles Herald* indicated the value of Goldman's social essays: "With her little hammer she knocks upon our rock-ribbed prejudices and with her scalpel she neatly and cleverly lays bare some of our social sores; and while we shall not accept her heroic remedies she gives us some interesting ideas to think about."[43]

Chapter Four
Dramatic Criticism
Goldman's Interest in Literature

Emma Goldman's perception of the social significance of literature began early in her life. She read Turgenev's *Fathers and Sons,* Goncharov's *The Precipice,* and Chernyshevsky's *What Is To Be Done?* during her impressionable years in St. Petersburg. Moreover, it has been argued that "a large part of her later life was consciously patterned after Vera Pavlovna, the heroine of *What Is To Be Done?*"[1] Since it encouraged her revolutionary zeal as a young woman, Goldman always appreciated the didactic and inspirational powers of literature.

Her sojourn in Vienna in 1895–96 heightened her interest. A more sophisticated young anarchist, Stefan Grossman, lent her books and encouraged her interest in writers like Nietzsche, Ibsen, Hauptmann, and von Hoffmansthal, "who were hurling their anathemas against old values." In the United States she had already "read snatches" of their works in *Arme Teufel,* published by Robert Reitzel in Detroit, which was in her view the only German newspaper in the United States "that kept its readers in contact with the new literary spirit in Europe. What I had read in its columns from the works of the great minds that were stirring Europe only whetted my appetite."[2] In addition, she sought out lectures on modern prose and poetry as well as attending operas and plays.[3] Especially in the writings of contemporary dramatists like Ibsen, Strindberg, and Shaw, she found the literary illustration of her political philosophy. While she appreciated the aesthetic elements in literature, as her autobiography and her letters clearly reveal, the anarchist themes that she found stimulated her ideological interest and convinced her of literature's value as a propaganda tool to influence middle-class audiences.

Goldman's professional work with literature took three forms. First, as publisher and editor of *Mother Earth,* she printed poems, stories, and essays on literary topics. Second, she lectured regularly and with great success on literary topics. The lecture notes on Whitman and Chekhov survive, but reports by her and others indicate that additional topics included "Art in Relation to Life," "Art and Revolution," "Russian Literature," "Modern Drama," *"Chanticleer,"* and speeches on individual writers, including Ibsen and Strindberg. Third, by drawing from her lectures, Goldman produced her most substantive critical work, *The Social Significance of the Modern Drama,* and projected a book on Russian drama, which did not materialize because of the financial problems of the prospective publisher. Whether as editor, speaker, or literary critic, Goldman invariably selected works for publication and discussion with a clear ideological bias. To appreciate her propagandistic work with literature, we require an understanding of her literary theory, an examination of her editorial work, a consideration of her essay on the impact of modern drama, and finally, a scrutiny of her major critical effort, *The Social Significance of the Modern Drama.*

Literary Theory: Art and Literature as Elements in Revolution

Goldman believed that art in general and literature in particular were closely tied to the spirit of revolution in two ways. First, the creative urge was simply one manifestation of the individual's yearning for self-expression, the force that underlay the revolutionary spirit. The artistic spirit best reflected the "growing unrest" that would eventually lead to the "open road" of a new regenerated social order.[4] True artists, spurred by the creative spirit like Constantin in *The Seagull* (1896), were keenly sensitive to social problems and in tune with the human spirit. Thus, in expressing their own natures, they addressed broad human concerns. Strindberg, whom she much admired and whom she considered one of the four major modern dramatists, reflected this pattern clearly. Goldman felt that in search of his own truth he offended many people because he held up "his searching mirror to *their* sore spots."[5] Such scrutiny, though painful, was essential for social progress. As a result of this critical scrutiny, modern literature embodied "the spirit of universal ferment and the longing for social change."[6] The numerous critiques of marriage in literary works, for example, were strong evidence for her claim that the institution was moribund.[7] The individualism personified in strong characters in literature was also evidence of the growing revolutionary ferment. The insights that inspired Goldman's contemporary writers and informed their works were, in essence, reflections of a larger, dynamic revolutionary spirit.

Second, the situations and forces that mandated revolution provided the richest material for an artist. In addressing the social problems and individual yearnings of the day, the artist reached the highest levels of creative expression. Criticizing the "respectable bohemians" of the St. Louis Art Guild for their lack of contact with the "stress and agony of a real Bohemian life," Goldman concludes: "Life in all its variety of color, in all its fulness and wealth is art, the highest art. He who does not help to bring about such a life is not an artist, no matter if he can paint sunsets or compose nocturnes."[8] Its realistic concern with contemporary social issues made modern art distinct from and superior to earlier works. "Art for art's sake presupposes an attitude of aloofness on the part of the artist toward the struggle for life: he must rise above the ebb and tide of life. He is to be merely an artistic conjurer of beautiful forms, a creator of pure fancy. That is not the attitude of modern art, which is preeminently the reflex, the mirror of life."[9] In her discussion of Sudermann, she was even more explicit. "The function of the artist is to portray Life—only thus can he be true both to art and to life." Indeed, the more closely art was tied to the sources of revolutionary zeal, the greater it was as art. Russian literature was a prime example. "It is no exaggeration to say that in no other country are the creative artists so interwoven, so much at one with the people. . . . In fact, all the great Russian artists have gone to the people for their inspiration, as to the source of all life. That explains the depth and the humanity of Russian literature."[10]

Although she could be expected to admire realistic and naturalistic authors, Goldman did not feel that literature had to be literally representational to be significant. Literature could reveal social truths indirectly or symbolically. For example, Goldman thought Rostand's fabulous drama *Chanticleer* (1910) was "a scathing arraignment of the emptiness of our so-called wise and cultured, of the meanness of our conventional lies, the petty jealousies of the human breed in relation to each other." The message in a work was significant, not its surface features that might be abstract or symbolic rather than concrete and literal. Leonid Andreyev's allegorical drama *King Hunger* (1909), which Goldman summarizes in *The Social Significance of the Modern Drama* with almost no analysis, was "a message

revolutionary, deeply social in its scope, illumining with glorious
hope the dismal horizon of the disinherited of the earth." Similarly,
Gerhart Hauptmann's "poetic fairy tale," *The Sunken Bell* (1896),
is "a tragedy as rich in symbolism as it is realistically true—a tragedy
as old as mankind, as elemental as man's ceaseless struggle to cut
loose from the rock of ages."[11]

The close relationship between art and the revolutionary spirit
placed special demands on the artist. Quoting Strindberg, Goldman
avers, "The modern artist is . . . 'a lay preacher' popularizing the
pressing questions of his time. Not necessarily because his aim is
to proselyte, but because he can best express himself by being true
to life." In discussing a play by Tolstoy, she links his greatness to
his deep feeling for the grave problems of the time and to his close
relationship to the people. As the "powerful conscience of Russia,"
Tolstoy exposes "her crimes and evils before the civilized world."
John Galsworthy's attitude toward drama, which she quotes in her
introduction to the analysis of his works, corresponded closely with
her own. "I look upon the stage as the great beacon light of civilization, but the drama should lead the social thought of the time
and not direct or dictate it. The great duty of the dramatist is to
present life as it really is. A true story, if told sincerely, is the
strongest moral argument that can be put upon the stage. It is the
business of the dramatist so to present characters in his picture of
life that the inherent moral is brought to light without any lecturing
on his part."[12]

But Goldman deplored the situation that arose in Russia, where
artists became merely the mouthpieces of new powers. "If such a
debacle is to be avoided in the future, the cultural forces, while
remaining rooted in the economic soil, must yet retain independent
scope and freedom of expression. Not adherence to the dominant
political party but devotion to the revolution, knowledge, ability,
and—above all—the creative impulse should be the criterion of
fitness for cultural work."[13] Above all, art should avoid the political
jargon of the day. It should express the ideals of the revolution
using its own language, which need not contain the favored slogans
and phrases of zealots.

Goldman recognized the great potential of modern literature,
especially of drama, as propaganda to stimulate true internal and
external revolution. Both the radical and the conservative, she felt,
were ignorant of its immense value, unaware "that any mode of

creative work, which with true perception portrays social wrongs earnestly and boldly, may be a greater menace to our social fabric and a more powerful inspiration than the wildest harangue of the soapbox orator." George Bernard Shaw's plays, for example, were more effective than his direct prose propaganda. "As the propagandist Shaw is limited, dogmatic, and set . . . but Shaw the dramatist is closer to life—closer to reality, closer to the historic truth."[14]

Conservatives, she felt, could not appreciate the revolutionary influence of literature because they saw danger only in explicit propaganda, having long "been fed on the historic legend that it is only the 'rabble' which makes revolutions, and not those who wield the brush or pen." In contrast, radicals were insensitive to the power of literature because "the average radical is as hidebound by mere terms as the man devoid of all ideas." Such slogans as "bloated plutocrats" and "economic determinism" summed up "the symbols of revolt" for such people. The language of art, which embraces "the entire gamut of human emotions . . . often sounds meaningless to those whose hearing has been dulled by the din of stereotyped phrases."[15]

Of all literature, drama is most useful to the revolutionist. "Because it reflects all life and embraces every ramification of society, the Modern Drama, showing how each and all are in the throes of the tremendous changes going on, makes it clear that they must either become part of the process or be left behind."[16] Thus, drama is "the strongest and most far-reaching interpreter of our deep-felt dissatisfaction."[17] Equally important, drama has an impact on those "who need enlightenment as much as the workers, the professional middle-class men and women who are only now beginning to buck up against life and who by training and habit are utterly unfitted for the shock." In America, where oppression has largely been felt only by the common people, drama is a perfect medium "to arouse the intellectuals of this country to make them realize their relation to the people, to the social unrest and to the brutalities and abuses going on day after day in this wide land."[18] In short, contemporary drama is an effective means of unifying the intellectuals and comfortable middle class with the proletariat in what should be their common revolutionary struggle. Thus, art teaches the bourgeoisie what the proletariat already know. Those who have learned "the great truths of the social travail in the school of life, do not need the message of the drama," Goldman writes, "but there is another class whose number is legion, for whom that message is indispensable." Because modern drama has the ability to rouse such groups to recognition of institutional and cultural injustices, its social significance makes it "the dynamite which undermines superstition, shakes the social pillars, and prepares men and women for the reconstruction."[19] Literature's ability to dramatize societal ills and to unify the masses is crucial to social change, because a successful revolution requires the participation and support of all groups: "The scientist, the engineer, the specialist, the investigator, the educator, and the creative artist, as well as the carpenter, machinist and the rest, are all part and parcel of the collective force which is to shape the revolution into the great architect of the new social edifice." Goldman's belief that social revolution requires the efforts of both intellectuals and workers was confirmed in Russia, where, she contended, Lenin had strategically polarized these groups to increase his own centralized power.[20]

Thus, in Goldman's mind, modern art and revolution were interdependent and, indeed, inseparable. Although she deplored narrowly propagandistic art from her ideological opponents, she insisted that the best works must reflect "social truths" and inspire revolution. Her practices as a publisher and literary critic clearly reflected this attitude.

Mother Earth: Goldman as Publisher

Goldman hoped that *Mother Earth* would provide a meeting ground for art and social criticism, for she wanted "to publish a magazine that would combine my social ideas with the young strivings in the various art forms in America." She saw the magazine as a complement to her other activities as well as an opportunity for young artists. "The spoken work, fleeting at best, was no longer to be my only medium of expression, the platform not the only place where I could feel at home. There would be the printed thought, more lasting in its effect, and a place of expression for the young idealists in art and letters. . . . They should speak without fear of the censor. Everybody who longed to escape the rigid moulds, political and social prejudices, and petty moral demands should have a chance to travel with us in *The Open Road.*" Even this first choice for a name suggested her aims, for not only did it evoke the image she sought but it was borrowed from Walt Whitman, who embodied the spirit of defiance and innovation she admired. When publishers of a periodical in Colorado objected to her choice of a title that they were already using, she turned to *Mother Earth,* which reflected her philosophy in its reference to the intimate relationship between liberated humans and nature. She summarized her goals for the magazine in its masthead: "Monthly Magazine Devoted to Social Science and Literature."[21]

The magazine, which included poems, reviews, and literary essays, did provide some exposure for young artists and a forum for the discussion of literary topics. Issues frequently began with a poem, sometimes from obscure poets but occasionally from established authors like Ibsen and Whitman. Her friend Max Baginski, who shared her interest in literature, contributed essays on "The Old and the New Drama" (April 1906), on "Gerhart Hauptmann's *The Weavers*" (February 1916), on "August Strindberg" (March 1914), and on "Three Plays by Brieux" (April 1912). Articles by others on Ibsen and "The Revolutionary Spirit in French Literature" appeared in early issues.[22] She also published commentaries on Edgar Lee Masters, Friedrich Nietzsche, Gustave Flaubert, and Ralph Waldo Emerson.[23] Inspirational excerpts from European writers like Zola, du Maupassant, Nietzsche, Byron, Kipling, Tolstoy, Voltaire, and Dostoyevsky and selections from Thoreau, Whitman, Emerson, and Lanier appeared intermittently.

The magazine did not live up to Goldman's projections, however. A survey of the literary essays, poems, and stories that she published reveals the problem. The pieces have thematic unity but lack consistent literary merit. The selections from major figures like Byron, Kipling, Ibsen, Tolstoy, and Dostoevsky all treat the political themes of freedom, social abuse of the individual, and anarchist theory. For example, a piece by Tolstoy examined "Law and Its Lies" (September 1916) and another by du Maupassant concerns "War—The Triumph of Barbarism" (September 1914). A short piece by Dostoyevsky, "The Priest and the Devil" (January 1909), so clearly expressed Goldman's views on prisons that she also incorporated it as the introduction to her essay on that subject. The selections from more obscure literary figures reflect the same limitations. A sampling of titles of fiction illustrates the thematic tenor: "Hymns of the War Kings" (February 1915); "The Revolt of the Ragged" (October 1913); "The Song of the Wage Slave" (May 1911); "The Chain

Gang: A Sketch" (October 1907); and "The Midnight Lunch Room" (July 1909).

Several factors explain *Mother Earth*'s limitations as a literary innovator. First, its precarious financial situation mandated a reduction from sixty-four pages to thirty-two, leaving less space for literary endeavors. Because its readership, estimated to be from 3,500 to 10,000 at most, never supported the cost of its publication, Goldman had to undertake lecture tours to continue on even this modest scale, thus leaving Berkman in charge for long periods. Berkman wanted to concentrate on a working-class audience and probably did little to seek out and encourage young artists, for "Berkman's interests were almost completely devoted to political and economic struggles—strikes, demonstrations, the problem of political prisoners."[24] As a result, under Berkman's editorship, literary topics and selections were shelved for the magazine's increased focus on social and political commentary. For example, the July and November issues of 1910 devote no space to literary matters, nor do the July and November issues of 1911. While such lapses are understandable, they also undercut the magazine's avowed purpose of attracting and opening avenues of expression to young writers.

Moreover, other less tendentious journals were available to aspiring writers. Margaret Anderson's *Little Review,* which was advertised in *Mother Earth,* was more attractive to young writers looking for a less politically narrow periodical. Even for radical writers and artists, the specifically anarchist bent of the magazine was a disincentive. As Wexler notes, during this period in the United States radical artists were drawn to socialism, not anarchism, and *The Masses,* not *Mother Earth,* "reaped their talent."[25] Consequently, no writer now considered important was first published in *Mother Earth.*[26]

The magazine's failure to publish significant experimental works is also traceable to its primary criterion of selection: a work had to reflect ideas implicit in anarchist theory. Literary merit and artistry were less important than ideology for acceptance for publication in *Mother Earth.* Goldman was often able to discriminate esthetically "good" from "bad" literature. With little training or formal education, her sensitivity to language and her intelligence led her to relish Shaw, Ibsen, Strindberg, and Whitman. As a professional propagandist, however, she looked at literature primarily for its social message rather than for its artistic merits. Richard Drinnon notes with a pleasingly ironic phrase that "her method amounted to little more than homily-hunting."[27] Thus, Goldman's motivations in *Mother Earth* were mixed: she longed to publish talented young authors, but if and only if they reflected her political theories and social views.

Goldman herself offered a related explanation, although in typical fashion she shifted the blame to the other side. After eight years of publication, she acknowledged that her initial naive assumption that the magazine would attract abundant appropriate contributions had been proved false. As she explained it: "The original purpose of gathering brave spirits who could find no expression in other periodicals has not materialized. Partly because brave spirits are scarce in this wide land; partly because those who are brave often cannot write, and mainly because those who are brave and can write, are compelled to write for money. *Mother Earth* is too poor to pay."[28] Consequently, the periodical had been hard pressed to find essays that met both its ideological and literary standards.

Wexler cites two other reasons for *Mother Earth*'s lack of success, both related to Goldman's editorial preferences. First, despite her avowed enthusiasm for innovative approaches, Goldman's literary tastes were largely conservative. Drawn to nineteenth-century realism, she disliked such technically innovative writers as D. H. Lawrence, James Joyce, and Gertrude Stein. Certainly, her critiques of plays reveal a keen interest in message at the expense of literary technique. What she sought, in essence, was radical ideology in conservative literary form. In addition, the persons most closely involved with her in writing for and producing the magazine lacked the background to stimulate literary experimentation. Although all of them were onetime activists and many had written for other radical periodicals, they lacked, in Wexler's terms, the sophistication, exuberance, and ease of people associated with other more successfully innovative periodicals. Thus, the editorial staff of *Mother Earth* lacked both the enthusiasm for and the knowledge of literary innovation that would have made the periodical more nearly what Goldman envisioned.[29]

If *Mother Earth* became a "distinguished gadfly," its realm was political rather than literary.[30] As one critic noted, "Along with *The Masses* and *The Liberator,* Miss Goldman's magazine influenced liberal thinkers to take a standard somewhat left of center in their attitudes toward the first World War and other contemporary issues."[31] Although *Mother Earth* may be dismissed as a direct stimulus to literary innovation, it perhaps made a subtler contribution. By publicizing radical ideas, advertising Goldman's lectures on drama, and including literary pieces alongside its political and social critiques, the magazine projected the role of literature in society. It undoubtedly acquainted many of its readers with the thoughts and contributions of literary figures, and the artistic efforts that it included, although sentimental and narrow to an experienced observer, probably offered a new perspective on both the problems of society and the relevance of literature to solving those difficulties. In connecting literature with real life, *Mother Earth* made an important contribution to the artistic community. It also introduced many literary figures to radical ideas because they respected Goldman's attention to the arts and were intrigued by her personality. [32]

Aside from the periodical itself, Goldman's Mother Earth Publishing Company was an important activity. In addition to reprinting her essays for distribution or sale at meetings, it printed works of other radical writers like Peter Kropotkin, Voltairine de Cleyre, and Margaret Sanger. It also offered copies of plays by Andreyev, Gorky, and Strindberg to its readers, sometimes as an incentive to resubscribe and sometimes as gift suggestions for Christmas. Of special note was her publication of Berkman's *Prison Memoirs of an Anarchist,* a work of considerable merit.

Goldman's Dramatic Criticism

Although Goldman lectured and wrote on many subjects, her talks on drama were among her most popular and most frequent. In a 1913 report in *Mother Earth,* Reitman observed that her lectures on literature were eclipsing those on economics. [33] But before the publication of *The Social Significance of the Modern Drama* in 1914, Goldman published very few essays on the subject. A review of a play by Eugene Walter, *The Easiest Way,* which appeared in 1909, and a general essay on drama in her collection *Anarchism and Other Essays* are her only pieces of dramatic criticism other than her book. But the impact of her work on drama among radical American intellectuals and the fact that her interest in literature distinguished her from other anarchist agitators make her efforts noteworthy. To appreciate Goldman's dramatic criticism requires an understanding of her attitude toward modern drama as she expressed it in her essay for *Anarchism and Other Essays,* which is an overview of her perspective. Then we can appreciate and assess her critical method and the analyses of particular dramas that she offers in her book.

"The Modern Drama: A Powerful Disseminator of Radical Thought"

The final piece in *Anarchism and Other Essays,* this well-organized and clearly argued essay both presents Goldman's analysis of the role of modern drama in producing revolutionary change and reinforces the social criticisms she has developed earlier in the book. In tracing the development of drama focused on social problems, Goldman relates particular plays to the abuses she has highlighted in earlier essays. The essay becomes, thus, not only a summary of the themes she has developed throughout the book, but also an optimistic assessment of the growth of revolutionary thought throughout society.

Goldman begins the essay by noting that when "discontent and unrest make themselves but dumbly felt within a limited social class, the powers of reaction may often succeed in suppressing such manifestations." When such feelings extend to other groups and begin to affect all dimensions of life, "the gradual transvaluation of existing values" becomes a reality. Unfortunately, such extension of revolutionary ferment cannot come merely from directly didactic political propaganda. Art, literature, and "above all, the modern drama—the strongest and most far-reaching interpreter of our deep-felt dissatisfaction" are the best vehicles for arousing widespread revolutionary sentiments. Although visual art and all literature are useful in this task, the modern drama, "as the leaven of radical thought and the disseminator of new values . . . has succeeded in driving home great social truths generally ignored when presented in other forms."[34]

With this theory in mind, Goldman then traces the role of drama in raising social consciousness throughout various nations. Russia and France are exceptions to her generalization, because other forces and traditions in those countries stirred revolution before the modern drama exerted its influence. Even in those countries, however, the works of writers like Tolstoy and Brieux "have undoubtedly reached wider circles than most of the articles and books which have been written . . . on the social question." In a preview of her organization within the essay, she asserts: "In countries like Germany,

Scandinavia, England, and even in America—though in a lesser
degree—the drama is the vehicle which is really making history,
disseminating radical thought in ranks not otherwise to be reached"
(243–44).

In Germany, her first example, persons of integrity and vision
had tried for a quarter of a century to awaken the social conscience.
"Alas! The cultured people remained absolutely indifferent; to them
that revolutionary tide was but the murmur of dissatisfied, discon-
tented men, dangerous, illiterate trouble-makers, whose proper place
was behind prison bars." At last, the work of Arno Holz, particularly
his *Familie Selicke* (1890) attracted attention and stimulated thought.
His graphic depiction of "society's refuse, men and women of the
alleys, whose only subsistence consists of what they can pick out of
the garbage barrels," aroused indignation because "truth is bitter,
and the people living on the Fifth Avenue of Berlin hated to be
confronted with the truth." The work of Sudermann also dealt with
vital subjects and pricked the German conscience. Gerhart Hauptmann, however, was "the dramatist who not only disseminated
radicalism, but literally revolutionized the thoughtful Germans"
(245, 248).

In her discussion of Hauptmann's works, Goldman identifies
themes that mirror her earlier discussions. *Before Sunrise* (1889), for
example, focuses on the "indiscriminate breeding of children by
unfit parents" and *The Weavers* (1892) helps "to rouse the consciousness of the oppressed" to the abuses they were suffering from
capitalism, which "cannot get far unless it devours labor." *The
Sunken Bell* portrays the tragedy of those who yearn for freedom and
change but are unable to achieve it because they lack "the strength
to defy venerated traditions." In the works of two other Germans,
Goldman perceives discussions of how Puritanism and its "dense
ignorance" frustrate the child's development and produce personal
tragedy (251).

Like the Germans, the Scandinavians had ignored the essays and
diatribes of reformers until Ibsen opened their eyes with his powerful
dramas. The plays of Ibsen that Goldman singles out for brief
discussion reflect basic themes in her revolutionary ideology. *Pillars
of Society* (1877) is a "tremendous indictment against the social
structure that rests on rotten and decayed pillars—pillars nicely
gilded and apparently intact, yet merely hiding their true condition." *A Doll's House* (1879) "paved the way for woman's emanci-

pation" and *Ghosts* (1881) exposes the falseness and even malevolence of notions like duty and obligation in human lives. In *An Enemy of the People* (1882), Ibsen "performs the last funeral rites over a decaying and dying social system. Out of its ashes rises the regenerated individual, the bold and daring rebel" (253–59).

England provides the final European example of Goldman's thesis. Shaw and Galsworthy are among those writers who have, in a relatively short time, "carried radical thought to the ears formerly deaf even to Great Britain's wondrous poets." A long quotation from Undershaft in Shaw's *Major Barbara* (1907) endorses Goldman's analysis of poverty as the greatest crime in society, her insistence on the delusion inherent in elections, and her urging of the necessity for radical action to make significant social changes. In part Undershaft asserts: "When you vote, you only change the name of the cabinet. When you shoot, you pull down governments, inaugurate new epochs, abolish old orders, and set up new." Although she did not accept this violent prescription for revolutionary change, Goldman did approve of Shaw's call for a new social order. Galsworthy's play *Strife* (1909) was, with Hauptmann's *The Weavers,* the most significant labor drama. Particularly "marvelous" and "brilliant," she argues, are its portrayal of the mob "in its fickleness and lack of backbone." Another work by Galsworthy, *Justice* (1910), confirms her view of the "grave social wrong" in prisons; and its practical impact in arousing concern about the issue in England bore out her thesis on the value of the drama (260–62).

The United States, she argues, is "still in its dramatic infancy" and "the only real drama" it has produced thus far is Eugene Walter's *The Easiest Way,* a work exploring the "criminal waste of human energy in economic and social conditions," which drives a woman to marry for security and encourages a fatalism that finally makes her "a parasite, an inert thing." A few other pieces pointed to a dawning of American drama, an art on the edge of "discovering to the people the terrible diseases of our social body" (270–71).

Having completed her survey demonstrating the pervasive influence of drama in various countries and having drawn attention to the recurrent themes she saw expressed in plays, Goldman concludes the essay with an affirmation of her faith in the growing revolutionary spirit. She also reiterates her view of how vital she feels modern drama is in this process: "Above all, the modern drama, operating through the double channel of dramatist and interpreter, affecting as it does both mind and heart, is the strongest force in developing social discontent, swelling the powerful tide of unrest that sweeps onward and over the dam of ignorance, prejudice, and superstition" (271).

This essay, which outlines the views Goldman developed in much greater detail in her book of dramatic criticism, is an effective survey of the previous essays in the collection. Indeed, it helped her to develop the underlying thesis of *Anarchism and Other Essays:* that anarchism provided the antidote for the problems she perceived in society. Drama was the means for conveying those problems to groups unfamiliar with them in a way that would move them emotionally and, finally, intellectually. As an educational tool, drama was part of the mechanism for peaceful social change that Goldman advocated.

The Social Significance of the Modern Drama

Despite Goldman's keen interest in drama and her frequent lectures on it, she might never have published a book on the subject except for a happy accident. A young stenographer, Paul Munter, presented her with a neat typescript of a lecture series she had presented.[35] As Goldman acknowledged, this draft tremendously simplified her task in preparing the work for publication. Berkman, then as later, was her helpful editor, and the book appeared in 1914 at the price of one dollar. In her autobiography she recalled her general satisfaction with the book when it was published and added, "My only regret was that my own adopted land had to be left out. I had tried diligently to find some American dramatist who could be placed alongside the great Europeans, but I could discover no one. Commendable beginnings there were by Eugene Walter, Rachel Crothers, Charles Klein, George Middleton, and Butler Davenport. The dramatic master, however, was not yet in sight."[36]

General approach. *The Social Significance of the Modern Drama* is divided into six sections: Scandinavian, German, French, English, Irish, and Russian. Goldman's preference for European drama is a manifestation of her focus on social criticism. American drama was, she felt, only in its nascent stages, although Eugene Walter's play *The Easiest Way* impressed her as an encouraging exception. Arguing that literature was an index to a nation's development, she asserts: "If so, we must assume that America had hitherto neither culture nor development, since its drama, at least, was of the poorest quality indeed. The people at large still consider the theater a place of cheap amusement and relaxation from the daily grind, while the melodramatic impossibilities serve as a vehicle to inflame the imagination of the street gamin or the hero worship of the boarding school miss."[37]

Although her rationale for choosing the countries is not explicit, her comments introducing some sections indicate that the area made a particular contribution to the development of modern drama or was in a crucial stage in its growing literary awareness. German drama, for example, had stultified during Prussian military success. After the Franco-Prussian War, "the country of poets and thinkers remained, intellectually, a veritable desert, barren of ideas. . . . Nothing thrived in Germany during that period, except a sickening patriotism and sentimental romanticism, perniciously misleading the people and giving them no adequate outlook upon life and the social struggle."[38] In this environment, the work of Hermann Sudermann and Gerhart Hauptmann marks an important awakening and offers strong evidence of the dynamic spirit of revolution sweeping Europe. Ireland's literary renascence is proof that "neither God nor King can for long suppress the manifestation of the latent possibilities of a people" (250). England, which was at the time the most productive nation in terms of dramatic art, was a clear indicator of "the power of modern drama as an interpreter of the pressing questions of the time" (196). In essence, Goldman uses her choice of nations to suggest the stages and success of revolutionary fervor. By implication, America, which had produced no dramatist worthy of inclusion although it was the market for her book, was retarded both artistically and politically.

Her criteria for choosing authors are more directly expressed. While most authors were chosen because a particular work develops a theme close to Goldman's heart, she singles out five men for more detailed treatment and discusses three or four of their works rather than the more customary one or two. They were selected because they provided particular slants on anarchist philosophy. Although she highlights Ibsen, Strindberg, Hauptmann, and Tolstoy as the men who "illumined the horizon of the nineteenth century," John Galsworthy also receives unusual consideration (87). Ibsen, who is the first author considered, is, Goldman feels, the "uncompromising demolisher of all false idols and dynamiter of all social shams and hypocrisy" (11). As an iconoclast, however, Ibsen remains aloof and deals with only one aspect of the human condition (88). Strindberg, the second author whom she treats, is "a keen dissector of souls," who "hated all artifice with all the passion of his being" (44). His scathing criticism of people, however, is sometimes "bitter" in contrast to Hauptmann, who was the most human, . . . also the most universal. . . . Hauptmann embraces, understands all, and portrays all, because nothing human is alien to him" (87). Although Goldman discusses only one play by Tolstoy, she extols him as a great crusader and insists that he escaped the fate of other outstanding Russians only because "he was mightier than the Church, mightier than the ducal clique, mightier even than the Tsar." Writing a work as powerful as his play *Power of Darkness* (1889) requires not only the vision of a creative artist, but "it requires a deeply sympathetic human soul. Tolstoy possessed both" (88, 276, 282). Galsworthy, who was the most prolific of English dramatists and whose work was comparable only to Hauptmann's, is "neither a propagandist nor a moralist. His background is life, 'that palpitating life,' which is the root of all sorrow and joy." The focus and his commitment to portraying life faithfully make him "thoroughly human and universal" (196–97).

The other writers whom Goldman considers are more important for particular themes or plays than for the scope of their writing. Shaw, for example, who was sometimes dismissed as a social dramatist because of his light touch, is noteworthy because his humor is the kind that "eats into the soul like acid, leaving marks often deeper than those made by the tragic form." His rather heavy-handed propagandistic approach, she feels, is necessary "because of the indolence of the human mind, especially the Anglo-Saxon mind, which has settled down snugly to the self-satisfied notion of its purity, justice, and charity, so that naught but the strongest current of light will make it wince" (175–76). Among the French, Brieux is one among "the few who treats the question (of venereal disease) in a frank manner, showing that the most dangerous phase of venereal disease is ignorance and fear" (148). Yeats, despite his avowed distaste for topical drama in *Where There is Nothing* (1904), offers "as true an interpretation of the philosophy of Anarchism as could be given by its best exponents" (252).

Although Goldman offers no concrete biographical information about the authors she treats, she often cites their avowals of their dedication to social change and their view of their art as portraying life or as stirring revolutionary sentiments. For example, Goldman begins her essay on Ibsen with a quotation from a letter he wrote after the Paris Commune, which revealed his attitude toward the state, an attitude that paralleled her own: "The State is the curse of the individual. How has the national strength of Prussia been purchased? By sinking of the individual in a political and geographical formula. . . . The State must go! That will be a revolution which will find me on its side. Undermine the idea of the State, set up in its place spontaneous action, and the idea that spiritual relationship is the only thing that makes for unity, and you will start the elements of a liberty which will be something worth possessing" (11). It is little wonder that Goldman admired Ibsen's analysis of society. In introducing *The Awakening of Spring* (1891) by Frank Wedekind, "perhaps the most daring dramatic spirit in Germany," Goldman mentions that he called the play "a tragedy of Childhood, dedicating the work to parents and teachers" (118). Shaw provided a clear description of his agenda in writing plays, which coincided with Goldman's artistic theories: "I am not an ordinary playwright in general practice. I am a specialist in immoral and heretical plays. My reputation has been gained by my persistent struggle to force the public to reconsider its morals. I regard much current morality as to economic and sexual relations as disastrously wrong; and I regard certain doctrines of the Christian religion as understood in England to-day with abhorrence. I write plays with the deliberate object of converting the nation to my opinion on these matters" (175). Galsworthy's view of drama as a leader of social thought and of the artist's role as a portrayer of life who should convey moral inspiration was also most congenial to Goldman's purpose (196–97). This testimony, by the authors themselves, undergirds the book's central thesis about the social significance of drama.

Because Goldman's aim was to demonstrate the role of drama in presenting and analyzing significant social problems, it is not surprising that her discussion of plays echoes the same themes she had expressed in her collected essays. Among the motifs she perceived in modern plays were the deleterious impact of artificial social constraints on individuals, the deplorable conditions confronting the oppressed, and the wickedness of existing institutions. Several plays have themes that correspond to specific topics addressed in her earlier essays: the abuses of the penal system, the need for the psychological emancipation of women, the danger of sexual ignorance, and the thwarting of children's development.

Critical method. In analyzing a play, Goldman concentrated on two features: (1) its plot as a depiction of the social problems she perceives and/or (2) the characters as they display (or fail to display) the individualism central to her anarchism. She paid no attention to such literary features as style, adequacy of plot, or character development. Her analysis of Ibsen's works, the longest section in the book, provides a representative example of her methodology.

Goldman begins with the excerpt from Ibsen's letter cited previously in which he attacks the notion of the state and avows his overriding concern for individual liberty. She continues: "The state was not the only *bete noire* of Henrik Ibsen. Every other institution which, like the state, rests upon a lie, was an iniquity to him. Uncompromising demolisher of all false idols and dynamiter of all social shams and hypocrisy, Ibsen consistently strove to uproot every stone of our social structure." Above all, she stresses, Ibsen thunders "against the four cardinal sins of modern society: the Lie inherent in our social arrangements; Sacrifice and Duty, the twin curses that fetter the spirit of man; the narrow-mindedness and pettiness of Provincialism, that stifles all growth; and the Lack of Joy and Purpose in work which turns life into a vale of misery and tears" (13, 18, 24, 34).

Goldman then traces these "Leitmotifs," as she terms them, through four of Ibsen's plays. She does not justify her choice of these plays in preference to others. In each discussion, she focuses on the particular "sins" treated in the play. *Pillars of Society* explores "the disintegrating effect of the Social Lie, of Duty, as an imposition and outrage, and of the spirit of Provincialism, as a stifling factor"; *A Doll's House* treats the social lie and duty; *Ghosts* touches on all except provincialism; and *An Enemy of the People* is "a powerful arraignment of the political and economic Lie" (23–24). To substantiate her interpretations, Goldman provides a synopsis of each play and quotes passages that convey the key points. For example, she quotes Nora's speech in *A Doll's House*, in which Nora asserts the primacy of her obligation to become a full human being over her roles as wife and mother (17). The inclusion of specific quotations not only reinforces Goldman's interpretations, but also conveys the flavor and force of the drama she is treating.

Goldman's summaries, however, often gloss over elements in the plot that do not correspond to her philosophy. For example, in her treatment of *Pillars of Society,* she does not examine the ramifications of Consul Bernick's retaining his control at the end of the play. Instead, she suggests unconvincingly that he was coming to a consciousness of himself (17). Other less ideological critics have been troubled and confused by the ending, which seems inappropriate to other elements in the play.[39] Goldman's listeners often admired her skill at "simplifying" dramatic structure, however. As one observer reported, "Emma Goldman's appreciation and interpretation of the Modern Drama are keen and powerful, for she reaches the profundity of each work, possessing as she does the gift of dispersing with masterful strokes the haziness created by intricate detail of plot and pointing out the universality of the big message beyond it all."[40] Clearly, Goldman's penchant for drawing out the details of plot that fit her theories impressed her audience despite its occasional interpretive oversimplification.

In her treatment of Ibsen's plays, Goldman also describes how certain characters grow in self-awareness and individualism as they confront the social forces she deplores. For example, Dr. Stockmann learns that the majority, though powerful, is not necessarily right and that "the strongest man is he who stands most alone" (41). Nora, closing the door of her doll's house, "opens wide the gate of life for woman and proclaims the revolutionary message that only perfect freedom and communion make a true bond between man and woman" (25). The changes in the characters are important, of course, not because of their individual development, but because of the universal social truths they embody or embrace.

Goldman concludes by explicitly linking Ibsen's merit to his social message. Without his revolutionary theories, she asserts, his dramatic art would be inconceivable. Furthermore, she argues, "his art would lose human significance were his love of truth and freedom lacking." The presence of these elements constitute "Henrik Ibsen's bugle call, heralding a new dawn and the birth of a new race" (42).

Limitations of Goldman's Dramatic Criticism

The overview of her treatment of Ibsen reveals some characteristic weaknesses in Goldman's criticism. Although her lectures were extremely popular with her audiences and apparently enlightening to them, several serious flaws limit their value as literary criticism:

(1) a narrow principle for selecting plays for consideration; (2) a failure to provide social or literary contexts for the works; (3) the limited standards of assessment that distort, truncate, and even misconstrue the essence of some plays; and (4) a failure to assess the relative merits of the works. Thus, although her analyses of dramas were propagandistically effective, the flaws are so substantial that they have little lasting value as literary criticism.

First, Goldman's eclecticism in selecting plays and playwrights for discussion is problematic. Her failure to justify her selections raises question about how typical and representative her choices are. If we assume that she chose those plays that supported her ideological biases, her thesis that the modern drama in general expressed growing revolutionary ferment is weakened. For example, by omitting any mention of *Uncle Vanya* (1899) and *The Three Sisters* (1901) in her treatment of Chekhov, Goldman not only distorts his attitude but probably overestimates the immediate social significance of his works as a whole. Her enthusiasm for the social message in William Butler Yeats's *Where There Is Nothing* leads her to overvalue what is generally regarded as an inferior play and to disregard Yeats's explicit repudiation of the "crude speculative commonplaces" in a scene she particularly admired.[41] More knowledgeable readers, recognizing that her selections are not adequately representative either of the works of individual authors or of modern drama altogether, quickly become skeptical of her generalizations.

Goldman often fails to provide adequate literary, personal, or social contexts for the works she discusses. To some extent, this information was outside her ken as a critic. Still, its omission limits the value of her criticism both in establishing her interpretive thesis and in indicating the social importance of the works she chooses. In at least two cases, Ibsen's *Pillars of Society* and Galsworthy's *Justice,* an explanation of the immediate social contexts would have enriched her analysis by revealing the specific social problems these plays were exploring.[42] Although Goldman alludes to the impact of Galsworthy's play in stimulating prison reform in her essay on drama in *Anarchism and Other Essays,* she does not explain the connection fully and omits any such reference in the section on Galsworthy in her book. Also, the absence of information about the work's literary context leaves readers unable to determine how innovative the work really was or what its place is in the author's canon. Because Goldman does not even provide dates of performance or publication, readers get little feel for the play's place in social or literary history. We are left uncertain about the breadth, depth, and even chronology of the literary developments Goldman perceived.

Her criticism overlooks so many aspects of individual dramas that the assessments seem truncated and even vacuous. At times she fails to follow up on important dimensions in plays that she herself notes. For example, she asserts that the Indian girl in *Pillars of Society* is a symbol of our society but does not elucidate nor elaborate (18). With Chekhov's plays she makes no mention of the symbolism that is closely intertwined with their messages.[43] Aesthetic merit that does not have easily perceived ideological import is consistently ignored. For example, focusing on the message in *Chanticleer,* Goldman ignores its skillful versification, although one modern critic notes: "The main defects of the work are to be found in the weak exposure of ideas. The play is too contrived, too far-fetched for presentation as a serious thesis work."[44] Goldman's commendation of the play, thus, focuses on one of its weakest elements.

More serious are omissions in her criticism that distort a work. For example, in her enthusiasm to commend Chanticleer as the idealist and the Pheasant Hen as "the eternal female . . . self-centered and vain," Goldman fails to mention the Pheasant Hen's heroic self-sacrifice at the play's end, an action designed to save Chanticleer.[45] An even more striking oversight appears in her view of Tolstoy's *Power of Darkness.* Seeing it as a gripping picture of misery and ignorance, Goldman fails to note what one critic terms "the truth of the play, its moral message of atonement for evil."[46] Indeed, Goldman quotes the son's plea for forgiveness from his father at the end, but does not cite the father's crucial response that God will forgive (282). Goldman's distaste for such Christian notions explains but cannot excuse her distortion of Tolstoy's Christianity.

In some essays her enthusiasm for one aspect of a play causes her to omit even the most basic elements from her critique. For example, in discussing Shaw's *Mrs. Warren's Profession* (1893) and *Major Barbara,* Goldman does not provide adequate plot summaries. In her treatment of *Mrs. Warren's Profession,* she does not reveal the outcome of the play nor delve into one central focus, the relationship between Mrs. Warren and her daughter. In her treatment of Andreyev's *King Hunger,* Goldman does not give an adequate overview of the plot, making her treatment of the play difficult to follow, because of her enthusiasm for the play's revolutionary theme. Readers are left uncertain of Andreyev's attitude toward King Hunger or the workers. Goldman's search for social significance in a drama that accorded with her philosophy sometimes blinded her to other views and subtler points. Her admiration for the individualism of David Roberts in *Strife* and his adamancy in pursuing his goals is at odds with a more penetrating and probable interpretation of the play as a plea for moderation and an indictment of such needless fanaticism. The implacability of Anthony and Roberts, which Goldman endorses, made them, for some critics at least, not heroes but "enemies of Society."[47] Although Goldman approved of such opposition to society, her analysis almost certainly oversimplifies Galsworthy's attitude. Moreover, Goldman's admiration for Roberts obscures Galsworthy's strong implied criticism of the labor movement.[48]

Her ideological commitment also causes her to overvalue some works. Despite their revolutionary themes, the works she treats by Stanley Houghton, Githa Sowerby, and T. G. Murray have sunk into deserved obscurity. Similarly, despite her enthusiastic predictions about the future of American drama under the leadership of Eugene Walter and Butler Davenport, they did not prove valuable in building a strong American repertoire.

One last weakness in Goldman's criticism is its lack of evaluation. Having chosen plays for their ideology, she praises that element in each and applies no other standard to distinguish among them. Admitting her enthusiasm for Ibsen, Strindberg, Tolstoy, and Hauptmann, she asserts, "It is unnecessary to make comparison between great artists: life is sufficiently complex to give each his place in the great scheme of things" (87). Although this stance is admirably egalitarian, it is not useful to those desirous of distinguishing among works of literature.

In reporting on a series of lectures that Goldman offered in Chicago, Margaret Anderson provided an explanation of the limitations in the talks that fits the essays as well. In Anderson's estimation, Goldman's attempt to cover too much territory in too little time caused her simply to summarize the play and comment on its social message. Although Goldman did this quite ably, Anderson felt that this approach made the discussions largely "uninteresting" because they failed to convey the spirit of Goldman's personality.[49] In other terms, we might note that Goldman's tendency to hunt for homilies reduced both the scope and depth of her criticism. The results are truncated, ideological statements rather than fully developed assessments.

The Value of Goldman's Criticism

Goldman's critical efforts, despite their weaknesses, have some strengths and values. If not a subtle critic, she nonetheless is intelligent and stimulating in many of her observations. George Middleton, reviewing her book in *La Follette's,* says, "It is not always necessary to agree with some of her social deductions, but no one can read the book without feeling its vigor and sincerity. . . . *The Social Significance of the Modern Drama* is a vital, soul-questioning volume which inquires rigorously into our social morality with courage and penetration."[50]

Despite her ideological bias, Goldman generally recognized excellence in literature. The playwrights she chose have considerable merit other than their anarchistic messages. So, while she was leading her audience to authors who expressed her views, she was, because of her own usually sound taste, conducting them to important literary figures and works.

Furthermore, for many works, her emphasis accords with the play's focus. Her interpretations, though limited, are often accurate. *A Doll's House* is, among other things, a critique of marriage and the roles women were compelled to play, just as Goldman observed. It does call for women to be aware of themselves as individuals before accepting other obligations. Goldman's perspective makes salient key features of this and other works. One critic, in comparing her analyses to other more literary efforts, notes that while she sometimes missed subtleties and lacked esthetic sensitivity, she was keenly alert to "basic truths about meanings and morals" that escaped others. Her works, thus, were sometimes useful in highlighting these concerns.[51]

Her interest in the meaning behind the plays rather than the surface details widens the range of plays that she could bring before her audience. Parables like Rostand's *Chanticleer* could be analyzed, as could starkly realistic pieces like Gorky's *A Night's Lodging (The Lower Depths),* (1912). Shaw's *Major Barbara* with its irony and humor could stand beside Ibsen's somber *Ghosts* as an examination of societal ills. Her search for meaningful plays was not chauvinistic;

she found examples in several countries. The diversity of homelands, authors, and plays is harmonized by the thematic unity she perceived. Thus Goldman served a valuable function in highlighting the universality of literary themes and in suggesting that good literature is not a respecter of geographic boundaries.

In her lectures and in her book, Goldman brought literature to many people who had no exposure to it. By emphasizing the treatment of social problems implicit in many plays, she made literature relevant to many of her audience's concerns. In a sense, she rescued literature from the popular perception that artists dwell in an ivory tower, and she made drama real for her audience. For many, Goldman's treatment of an art form as an exploration of practical problems opened new vistas. Her enthusiasm inspired many to study the works she discussed and others more thoroughly. Furthermore, her method of seeking a social message provided a framework within which even many untrained people could think about plays. Her wide sampling of authors, plays, and countries provided a literary smorgasbord from which her audience could choose topics, types, or authors that appealed to them. Some, who began reading because they were excited by the anarchism in the works, lingered to enjoy the poetry, the characterizations, and the plots Goldman often glossed over.

Goldman was also willing to examine works from new perspectives and to develop new interpretations. She was unfettered and unimpressed by other critics. For example, she defends Chekhov from critics who charged that his works provided no message or solutions to the problems he portrayed. His strength and value, she asserts, are his honest, empathetic characterizations of people caught in complex situations. His failure to suggest solutions "is not weakness in the artist, since in life there are no solutions unless they are arbitrarily created as in the conventional drama . . . and originality and truth in the artist are after all his most important characteristics."[52] In essence, Goldman's dramatic criticism is individualistic. Freely challenging earlier interpretations, she is unafraid of proposing new views and attitudes.

Goldman was not a voice crying in the wilderness of dramatic criticism, however. Other figures were examining the same materials as she, finding similar truths, and extolling like virtues. For example, Ashley Dukes's *Modern Dramatists*, published two years before Goldman's book, surveys eleven of the dramatists she covered and seven others.[53] Dukes, too, praises modern drama's search for truth and innovation, but he also explores the plays' literary features. Goldman's views, while novel and exciting to her audiences, were not unique on the critical scene. Others were communicating many of the same ideas. What is distinctive in Goldman's work is her extensive, frequent lectures on the drama. Although other books like Dukes's were available at that time, Goldman as a public lecturer on primarily political topics provided a real service to literature. The major value of her critical efforts is the unique combination of her format, her audience, her perspective, and her enthusiasm in addressing literary matters.

Chapter Five

Historical Works

The personal reactions of the participants and observers lend
vitality to all history.

—*My Disillusionment in Russia*

Although Goldman devoted most of her energies to social criticism
and to explanations of anarchism, she also produced two historical
works: *My Disillusionment in Russia* and *Living My Life*. Both are
primarily straightforward chronicles of events, but they differ in
their approach. Despite her disgruntlement over its suggestive title,
My Disillusionment in Russia is a narrative with an implicit argu-
mentative thesis: the Bolsheviks had betrayed the Russian Revolution. In contrast, *Living My Life* is a candid, although sometimes
tedious recital of Goldman's activities, with a focus on her involvement in the anarchist movement. Although her dedication to anarchism colors and constricts both, each offers insights into the
events it records and into Goldman herself.

My Disillusionment in Russia

Goal and purpose: The preface.   In undertaking to write candidly and, she hoped, fairly about her disillusionment in Russia,
Goldman faced two problems, which she discusses in her rather
lengthy preface. First, simply acknowledging the failure of the Bolshevik revolution to herself was extremely difficult because of her
early enthusiasm for the movement and her lifelong identification
with the struggles of the Russian people for freedom and social
change. As she expresses it:

The strongest of us are loath to give up a long-cherished dream. I had
come to Russia possessed by the hope that I should find a new-born country
with its people wholly consecrated to the great, though very difficult,
task of revolutionary reconstruction. And I had fervently hoped that I
might become an active part of the inspiring work. I found reality in

Russia grotesque, totally unlike the great ideal that had borne me upon the crest of high hope to the land of promise. It required fifteen long months before I could get my bearings. Each day, each week, each month added new links to the fatal chain that pulled down my cherished edifice. I fought desperately against the disillusionment. For a long time I strove against the still voice within me which urged me to face the overpowering facts. I would not and could not give up.[1]

With this very candid description of her struggle, Goldman, who had always railed against those whose thinking was controlled by myth or superstition, admits her vulnerability to these same forces.

Goldman's difficulty in coming to terms with the realities she perceived in Bolshevik Russia was exacerbated by her earlier support of Lenin and his fellow Marxists. Her decision to endorse the Marxists had come despite her theoretical differences with what she labeled a "cold, mechanistic, enslaving formula" (xliv). She had, in fact, issued a pamphlet, "The Truth About the Bolysheviki," that extolled the Marxists for adopting "Anarchist revolutionary tactics" and castigated her mentor Kropotkin and others, who did not support the Bolsheviks, for abandoning their lifelong anarchist ideals (xlv). In essence, by acknowledging her disillusionment Goldman was repudiating her earlier published views and retracting her rather ungenerous criticism of fellow anarchists.

Her second problem in undertaking to write about her observations was her realization that her account would be questioned because of her ideological differences with the Marxists. In particular she noted that some persons might disregard her perceptions because they felt that her focus on the individual and on personal liberty would make her intolerant of the repressive and even violent measures necessary for the Bolsheviks to establish revolutionary change. Goldman answered these anticipated objections by insisting, first, that she could have accepted the Bolsheviks' suppression of some individual rights "if the Russian workers and peasants as a whole had derived essential social betterment as a result of the Bolshevik regime." But, "try as I might I could find nowhere any evidence of benefits received either by the workers or the peasants from the Bolshevik regime" (xlvii–viii). She also admitted that she could accept the need for violence to usher in social change, but she felt that the Bolsheviks had made "a principle of terrorism," had "institutionalized" it and assigned it "the most vital place in the social struggle" (xlix). In her preface to the second portion of the book, published separately in the United States, she pointed out quite convincingly that by 1925, the date when she was writing, "the military fronts have long ago been liquidated; internal counter-revolution is suppressed; the old bourgeoisie is eliminated; the 'moments of grim necessity' are past" (liii). In short, the Bolsheviks had continued abusive policies beyond the time needed to establish revolutionary change.

Goldman stoutly maintains the fairness of her observations and the purity of her motivations in writing *My Disillusionment in Russia,* although she acknowledges that the work is subjective. "I do not pretend to write a history," she explains. "But the real history is not a compilation of mere data. It is valueless without the human element which the historian necessarily gets from the writings of the contemporaries of the events in question" (xliii). She intends to provide such a human account. She is particularly concerned that the reports being published even by well-intentioned persons were "most inadequate. They were written by people with no first-hand knowledge of the situation and were sadly superficial. Some of the writers had spent from two weeks to two months in Russia, did not know the language of the country, and in most instances were chaperoned by official guides and interpreters" (xliii). The "royal" treatment accorded the British delegation and the consequently distorted view of Russia they received are examples of the misin-formation she hopes to counteract (59). Goldman offers her account as one who had "shared the misery and travail of the people who actually participated in or witnessed the tragic panorama in its daily unfoldment" (xliii).

Moreover, she emphasizes that her motivations for writing the book are lofty: "I could do nothing for suffering Russia while in that country. Perhaps I can do something now by pointing out the lessons of the Russian experience. Not my concern only for the Russian people has prompted the writing of this volume: it is my interest in the masses everywhere" (1). At the conclusion of her preface to the volume containing the chapters that had been acci-dentally omitted in the first edition, Goldman adopts a familiar, somewhat martyred tone: "If my work will help in these efforts to throw light upon the real situation in Russia and to awaken the world to the true character of Bolshevism and the fatality of dic-tatorship—be it Fascist or Communist—I shall bear with equan-

imity the misunderstanding and misrepresentation of foe or friend.
And I shall not regret the travail and struggle of spirit that produced
this work, which now, after many vicissitudes, is at last complete
in print" (xlv–xlvi).

The narrative technique.   To develop her indictment and prove
her contention that "today . . . the Bolsheviki stand as the arch
enemies of the Russian Revolution," Goldman uses a straightforward
narrative interlaced with her reactions to events and experiences
(xliv). In effect, the events she chronicles are the raw material for
her musings and analysis, which lead to her final conclusion and
her decision to write the book. Thus, the book's organization is an
argument from generalization. Each episode adds evidence to the
claims that she is advancing.

The narrative is rich with the details of Goldman's life in Russia,
but the events are recorded, despite her claims, through the lens of
her lifelong political activitism. While she was probably honest
about her hopes for the success of the revolution, her ideological
commitment and her critical habit of mind make her always the
questioning and skeptical observer. In her attempt to base her conclusions closely on "reality," Goldman provides a myriad of details
that sometimes makes the narrative cumbersome. Her precise observations, however, provide some of the human elements that she
believed would be helpful for a later, more objective history.

Goldman's use of the chronicle to build a case against the Bolsheviks is clear in two examples. In reporting her first impressions
of Moscow, Goldman analyzes the poor institutional food she was
served as a symptom of Bolshevik corruption: "The food was not
too plentiful, but one could exist on it were it not so abominably
prepared. I saw no reason for the spoiling of provisions." A brief
visit to the kitchen revealed not only many cooks competing for
space and facilities but also discrimination. "The kitchen staff were
poorly paid; moreover, they were not given the same food served
to us. They resented this discrimination and their interest was not
in their work. The situation resulted in much graft and waste,
criminal in the face of the general food shortages. . . . Was that
communism in action, I wondered" (25). In this trivial incident,
Goldman intends to show the inequity, the bureaucracy, and the
inefficiency she saw as inherent in Bolshevism. The passage reflects
a typical pattern in the narrative: she moves from reporting an
activity (dining at a communal hall), to investigation of the problems

(the kitchen situation), to her general assessments and conclusions about its significance (Bolshevik communism is a fraud).

Later, in reporting her visit to Poltava as a representative of the Museum of the Revolution, she contrasts the spacious, well-equipped car in which the group traveled and which they were forbidden to share with the general delapidation of the railway system and the overcrowding of available trains. "At every station there was a savage scramble for a bit of space. Soldiers drove the passengers off the steps and the roofs, and often they had to resort to arms. Yet so desperate were the people and so determined to get to some place where there was hope of securing a little food, that they seemed indifferent to arrest and risked their lives continuously in this mode of travel" (122). Emma notes the great good humor of the people in the face of such problems, but speculates whether their inability for any "sustained effort" was not one reason for "the tragic condition of the Revolution" (124). With these observations of and musings about her train trip, Goldman as a reporter is constructing an indictment of Bolshevik inhumanity and a paean to the rich spirit of the Russian people. Her selection of details is the work of a political activist, constantly criticizing the system in operation.

In addition to describing her activities and experiences, Goldman frequently reports conversations with significant individuals, which confirm her views or provide evidence for her indictment. For example, an offhand remark by her Russian host on her first day in the country that compared the Marxist political organization to that of the infamous Tammany Hall in New York struck her as "discordant" and perplexed her, causing her to wonder about what was happening there (4). Her first meeting with Lenin was most illuminating to her. Although he tries to flatter her by commending her speeches at her trial for opposing the draft, which he had read, she refuses to be taken in. In contrast, his answer to her questions about the suppression of anarchist publications and the imprisonment of dissenters seems to her most revealing: "But as to free speech, . . . that is, of course, a bourgeois notion. There can be no free speech in a revolutionary period" (33). Her assessment of Lenin is devastating. "Free speech, free Press, the spiritual achievements of centuries, what were they to this man?" Labeling him "a Puritan" and "a shrewd Asiatic," she is "convinced that his approach to people was purely utilitarian, for the use he could get out of them for his scheme" (34). Her subsequent visit with Peter Kropotkin, whom she had castigated for being negative about the revolution, was equally revealing. Although she took no notes and could give "only the gist" of what he said, she carefully recites his analysis of the abuses of the Bolsheviks and his criticism of their approach. She is particularly distressed that Kropotkin has no plans for communicating his views to a larger public despite his strong misgivings. The thought that he might die before revealing his opinions on this topic is "appalling" (37). Rhetorically, such reported conversations add force to Goldman's analysis. Although we cannot assume that her reports are complete or necessarily factually accurate, we can see that within the book they build her credibility and strengthen her case.

The book, replete with these recalled conversations and significant events, always focuses on Goldman's almost instant, mounting suspicion of the Bolsheviks. From her first days, the simplest remarks and comments, even the contents of a meal ("good soup, meat and potatoes, bread and tea—rather a good meal in starving Russia, I thought") increase her disquietude (147). Many chapters begin or conclude with explicit references to her growing disillusionment, and her good faith attempts to stifle her disappointment. Seizing John Reed's rather puzzling last words, "caught in a trap," Goldman reflects at the end of one chapter: "In the face of death the man of mind sometimes becomes luminous: it sees in a flash what in man's normal condition is obscure and hidden from him. It was not at all strange to me that Jack should have felt as I did, as everyone who is not a zealot must feel in Russia—caught in a trap" (168). Another chapter, "Beneath the Surface," begins with her growing apprehensions. "The terrible story I had been listening to for two weeks broke over me like a storm. Was this the Revolution I had believed in all my life, yearned for, and strove to interest others in, or was it a caricature—a hideous monster that had come to jeer and mock me?" (68).

As her experiences reveal to her the true situation in Russia, Goldman's chronicling of events becomes more overtly critical. Her reports of the visitors who came to Russia for the Third Congress of the Third International, for example, are caustic. She is particularly critical of the American delegation, who were "most conspicuous by their lack of personality" (215). She portrays all the delegates as dupes of the Bolsheviks, who "know how to set the stage to produce an impression" (215). In the next chapter, "Ed-

ucation and Culture," Goldman abandons any chronological plan
to expose how the Bolsheviks have stifled creativity and, despite
some broadening of opportunities for the peasants, have mismanaged
education. The state's control of art, she claims, has "stultified the
cultural and artistic expression of the Russian people." She refutes
the Bolshevik claim that revolutionary periods are not conducive to
art by citing the French Revolution (224–25). As a consequence of
Bolshevik policies, she argues, "Russia is now the dumping ground
for mediocrities in art and culture. They fit into the narrow groove,
they dance attendance on the all-powerful political commissars. They
live in the Kremlin and skim the cream of life, while the real poets—
like Blok and others—die of want and despair." Only the Moscow
Art Theatre and Stanislavsky are exceptions (226–27). In every way,
the Bolsheviks have suppressed the "social phase of life in Russia"
because of their fears of counterrevolutionary ferment (231).

As the chapter on education and culture suggests, the problems.
Goldman perceived and the objections she raised to the Bolshevik
government paralleled many of those she had discussed in the United
States. Recurrent themes in her chronicle are the privileged treatment afforded to the party leaders at the expense of the masses, the
bureaucratic bungling that made life more difficult and wearying
for everyone, the repression of individual liberties, and the suppression of dissent. She castigates the Bolsheviks repeatedly for their
insensitivity to human beings and argues that the centralized state
under whatever ideology is destructive. In short, Goldman's selection of events and experiences to report reflects her lifelong concerns.

On another level, the book traces Goldman's psychological and
emotional journey during two very painful years. While she sometimes seems a bit superior in suggesting her sensitivity to and
perceptiveness about conditions, her inner turmoil is convincing.
As an idealist confronting the realities of revolution, she had to
reexamine her values and views: Was social change worth the painful
consequences she saw in Russia? Could revolution occur without
violence? How could a new order cope with the exigencies created
by the dissolution of one system and the creation of another? The
degree of turmoil these questions produced in her is clear from the
report of Angelica Balabanova in her autobiography *My Life as a
Rebel*. When Goldman visited her, Balabanova, a prominent Russian
revolutionary, recalled that Goldman broke into tears and "poured
forth all her shock and disillusionment, her bitterness at the injus-

tices she had witnessed, the others of which she had heard. . . . Was it for this that the Revolution had been fought?"[2] Reconciling these conflicts tormented Goldman; her idealism, her hopes for the success of the revolution clashed with the circumstances she saw: "I longed to close my eyes and ears—not to see the accusing hand which pointed to the blind errors and conscious crimes that were stifling the Revolution. I wanted not to hear the compelling voice of facts, which no personal attachments could silence any longer" (171). Caught between her aspirations for social revolution and the realities in Russia, Goldman felt responsible to inform workers, who might be misled by Russian propaganda, but was apprehensive that her testimony would be used against legitimate forces working for change. "For the first time in my life I refrained from exposing grave social evils. I felt as if I were betraying the trust of the masses" (172). Whatever its shortcomings as an historical report, *My Disillusionment in Russia* is noteworthy as a candid, poignant portrait of an idealistic, conscientious human being confronted with unpleasant, disillusioning realities.

Not surprisingly, reactions to the book were disappointing although not unexpected. Communists labeled her a traitor; most other liberals disregarded her conclusions.[3] The book's impact was also limited by the fact that other observers were issuing quite different assessments. H. L. Mencken, for example, reviewed it along with *The First Time in History: Two Years of Russia's New Life* by Anna Louise Strong, who drew completely different conclusions from a very similar exposure. Although Mencken acknowledged his preference for Goldman's book, noting that "behind her writing is a far finer and mellower intelligence," he asserted that the disparate conclusions simply reflected antithetical prejudices. Goldman's perspective, he felt, was too constrained by her aversion to any form of governmental control. She was "too indignant" when she perceived that the Bolsheviks, like all other people, were motivated by self-interest. Strong's interpretation of the same perception was much different. In fact, Mencken pointed out that "more than once, indeed, their statements of cold fact touch, kiss and almost coalesce."[4]

Goldman's book never had the force and impact she had hoped. It did not alert Western liberals to the "horrors" of the Bolsheviks. Their enthusiasm for the new Communist state and the glowing reports of groups who had been shown what she contended were unrepresentative showcases outweighed her efforts.[5] In truth, probably the public's perception of Goldman as an unrelenting critic of any attempt at social order and her reputation as a committed anarchist undercut her ethos as a dispassionate historian. She was easy to discredit and dismiss.

Living My Life

Although friends often urged Goldman to write her autobiography, other activities and financial pressures precluded it. Theodore Dreiser admonished her in Paris in 1926: "You must write the story of your life, E. G. . . . . It is the richest of any woman's of our century." He accompanied his statement with a promise to secure her an advance from a publisher.[6] Later, he reported he had been unsuccessful in his overtures to six publishers: "The thought of an honest radical seems to chill them to the marrow."[7] In her introduction to Living My Life, Goldman mentions her own hesitancy in undertaking to write her autobiography. Noting that suggestions like Dreiser's had come early when she "had barely begun to live," she adds that her deep involvement in the events around her and her belief that age would produce the detachment and philosophical perspective necessary for a meaningful autobiography made her refrain from undertaking such a project.[8] Her forced idleness at St. Tropez, however, changed her mind. Not only did she have the necessary leisure for the project, but her reading of other autobiographies had alerted her to the dangers of "senility, narrowness, and petty rancour" that accompanied old age (v). Thus, in 1928 she was willing to undertake the project.

Despite her readiness to begin, other obstacles had to be overcome. First, because her financial situation remained precarious, she lacked the funds to support herself during the interim. Fortunately, friends, including Dreiser, and her Canadian lecture tour in 1927–28 finally provided enough money to secure her the leisure to write. Another problem that at first seemed insurmountable was her "lack of historical data" for the work (v). Because her archives and all her personal papers had been seized by the United States government in 1917 and not returned, she had no record of many of her activities. Indeed, as she notes, "I lacked even my personal set of the Mother Earth magazine, which I had published for twelve years" (v). Again, her friends proved invaluable. Several did extensive research for her and provided the information she required. Especially noteworthy was Agnes Inglis, who had founded the Labadie Collection, now at the University of Michigan, which Goldman labeled "the richest collection of radical and revolutionary material in America" (vi). Friends also provided the "veritable mountains of letters" that she had written. These were essential in helping her recreate "the atmosphere of my own personal life: the events, small or great, that had tossed me about emotionally" (vi). The farsightedness and generosity of her friends soon provided her with "over one thousand specimens of my epistolary profusions," which though very painful to read, were "for my purpose . . . of utmost value" (v).

With both financial and historical resources at her disposal, Goldman confronted the task of reconstructing her past. The process proved extremely painful emotionally. She confided to Berkman in a letter that the recalling of relationships, which had meant so much and were now completely gone, was one of the most agonizing experiences of her life.[9] The resurrecting of the past and the attempt to express her reactions and explain her feelings proved both depressing and frustrating. A letter from St. Tropez in March 1929 to an American friend reveals her state of mind:

There is nothing new I can tell you about myself, except that I am struggling with my book. Sometimes it doesn't seem worth the pain it causes. What difference does it make whether people know about my life or not. I am not in the least deceived as to its importance. I know that when the book is finally turned over to the public there will be only a small minority who will appreciate the agony of soul that was mine during those years and even more so now in the process of reliving it. Frankly, if it were not for the beautiful spirit of a few people who are sustaining me during my efforts I would have thrown the whole damn thing overboard. I don't see why anyone should go through such an excruciating task unless the joy is commensurate. In my case it isn't. . . . For the rest, I have enough to carry me through until July. I don't know what will happen then but at present I am not giving it much thought. I have neither the time nor the strength—my writing consumes all I have.[10]

In the introduction to the work, Goldman also alludes to the emotional difficulties she confronted as she wrote. "Writing had never come easy to me, and the work at hand did not mean merely writing. It meant reliving my long-forgotten past, the resurrection of memories I did not wish to dig out from the deeps of my consciousness.

It meant doubts in my creative ability, depression and disheartenings" (vi–vii).

As Goldman struggled to record even painful events candidly, Berkman had the uncomfortable job of editing the work. According to his reports, she was often not amenable to his suggestions. Yet despite the tensions, their collaboration was successful.[11] Finally finishing in early 1931, Goldman wrote to a friend, "I do not know whether I have done a great or little thing, that is for my friends as well as enemies to decide when they read the book. I know I have done it as truthfully as is humanly possible."[12]

Purpose and technique. From the moment she agreed to write about her life, Goldman was determined to write both a personal and political narrative. As she wrote to her friend Hutchins Hapgood, "I want the events of my life to stand out in bold relief from the social background in America and the various events that helped to make me what I am: a sort of conjunction between my own inner struggles and the social struggles outside."[13] In one sense, Goldman wanted her book to be a record of an individual life dedicated to a cause, rather than a purely intimate recollection. To Berkman she wrote:

I am writing about the life of Emma Goldman, the public person, not the private individual. I naturally want to let people see what one can do if imbued with an ideal, what one can endure and how one can overcome all difficulties and suffering in life. Will I be able to do that and yet give also the other side, the woman, the personality in quest for the unattainable in a personal sense? That's going to be the rub. But I mean to do it.[14]

Because she felt that her personal and public lives were so closely related—"from the time I entered our movement I had no personal life which did not also reflect the movement, or my activities in it"—she was committed to including at least some of the more intimate details of her experiences.[15]

In writing such an account, Goldman was compelled to consider purely pragmatic problems. How frank could she be about her personal life without detracting from the political emphasis or becoming too titillating for her American audience? Her desire for the book to sell well enough to provide her with some much needed funds clashed with her realization that a fully frank autobiography would have little chance of being published.[16] Despite these res-

ervations, Goldman still felt it essential to convey the interplay
between her theories and her lived experiences. At the urging of
friends who believed that too much attention to her love life would
detract from her historical focus, she omitted some of the more vivid
details of her erotic escapades and discussed only "such cases, whether
of love or other events, that really went deep, or were of wide
scope."[17]

The decision to focus on the movement lead her to organize the
initial sections of the book to highlight her development as an
anarchist. Thus, she begins with her return to New York City in
1889 because she felt that was a turning point of her life. Details
of her previous years, especially her childhood, are interspersed in
the narrative when they pertain to her growing commitment to the
cause. Because her discussion of them is so intermittent and because
she spends so little time in analyzing her emotional and psychological development during her childhood, we get little sense of her
development as a person. As Waldo Frank notes in his review of
the book for the *New Republic,* "Intimately, for all her good will,
she appears to remember little of her own sensations. . . . I had
a sense of Emma Goldman writing these pages of her youth; but it
was a sense of the mature woman the author, not of the young
woman the subject."[18]

As the narrative develops, particularly in the early sections, Goldman interweaves discussions of her personal life, especially of her
sexual relationships, with reports of her political activities. The
reader perceives two related but distinct lines of development. As
an anarchist, Goldman moves from the innocent hopefulness of her
arrival as an immigrant in New York to a quick awareness of capitalistic abuses and to an attraction to radical politics. Under the
guidance of Most and Berkman, she becomes a close student of
anarchism and begins her earliest efforts as an agitator. As she
describes this progress, Goldman pays close attention to the details
of her growing involvement but gives few insights into her intellectual processes. For example, although she notes that her experiences in Blackwell Island Penitentiary provided her with a new
self-confidence and resolve, she does not explain clearly the forces
that produced this change. Indeed, as she traces her development
as an anarchist, the reader gets little sense of the stages of the process
because Goldman makes few distinctions between trivial occurrences
and more significant events. When she appears at the Amsterdam

conference in 1907 as a spokesperson for individualistic anarchism, the reader is almost surprised at her prominence and visibility.

Goldman's discussion of her publishing activities reveals her failure to provide helpful insights into her development quite clearly. In her progress as an anarchist, the establishment of *Mother Earth* is obviously a crucial event. Despite her mentions of the magazine, the autobiography provides little information about its operation and her role in it. Goldman spends very little space informing the reader about the uniqueness of the periodical or its editorial policies and practices. The same is true of the books she published. Aside from brief references to them, the reader learns little about their substance or the process of their development. Instead, Goldman provides details of her agitative activities and a chronicle of her numerous meetings and travels. What emerges in the pages of the autobiography is a record of what Goldman did rather than a description of what she thought.

On the second level, Goldman's depiction of her personal development focuses most closely on her sexual relationships. Although she does not provide a careful analysis of these, the reader can perceive her movement from relationships that mixed sexual desire and admiration (Most and Berkman) to more purely physical ones, perhaps best exemplified in Ben Reitman. This progress is suggested by Goldman's mentioning of books and intellectual conversations that she shared with her early lovers, while such episodes are rarer in her later affairs. Goldman's candor about her attractions to men is impressive, though perhaps a bit facile. In one sense, despite her insistence on her deep emotional involvements, she remains aloof and distant in her descriptions. Increasingly, her concern for her anarchist activities eclipses her focus on her affairs. Her liaison with Reitman, which came near her fortieth year, is a culmination of her sexual development, and incidents afterward have much less intensity and color.

Despite her intention to put her life against the backdrop of the larger social history, her narrative provides very little of the context necessary to understand events. Because her chronicle is so detailed and the activities of an unusually energetic person are so various, few episodes receive a full discussion. Often key figures and important episodes are treated so succinctly that the reader gets little sense of continuity or development. In particular, the events and activities in which she was involved are not clearly related to happenings on the broader social and political fronts. There is little attempt to integrate her personal history of anarchism with larger political currents or even to trace its course completely. Study of the individual chapters of the book reveals a detailed and often confusing amalgam of materials. Adhering strictly to chronology after the initial chapters, Goldman mixes the personal and the political, the important and the trivial without an attempt to synthesize or organize the materials more carefully. For example, the chapter that treats events after her release from prison and before her deportation moves from her confrontation with Reitman, to her musings on her mother and Helena during a family visit, to her acquaintance with a female revolutionary, to details of an operation on Berkman, to a report of her deportation hearing, then to her learning of the death of Frick. This crowded and jumbled assortment of events and impressions is both confusing and frustrating. Her close attention to details often obscures her assessment of important events.

The chapters on Goldman's experiences in Russia are perhaps the most interesting in the book. Because she focuses her attention more closely on the most significant occurrences, these chapters have a dramatic immediacy and force that other chapters lack. Perhaps her writing of the details of this experience earlier in *My Disillusionment in Russia* helped Goldman to perceive and highlight the essential aspects of the period. For whatever reason, this section and the record of her early days in New York are particularly appealing.

In her preface to *My Disillusionment in Russia,* Goldman expressed her intention of providing the "human record" of the impressions and reactions of an individual who had lived through a critical period. Such materials were, she felt, indispensable for later historians to write "real history." In a very real sense, her autobiography is another such document. It provides an insider's view of the activities of a significant social movement. The details of events and people she offers are certainly invaluable to anyone seeking to learn about early twentieth-century anarchism. In the same way, the work is a crucial starting point for anyone wishing to know about Goldman herself. Because of its scope and purpose, however, it is not definitive as either a history of anarchism or as a biography of Emma Goldman, although its richness and variety make it an important literary and historical document.

Assessment. As Dreiser notes, Goldman's life provided abundant material for an exciting, vibrant autobiography. Her intense involvement with controversial causes threw her into contact with many interesting people. Moreover, her own personality, a complex mixture of passion and reason, optimism and pessimism, compassion and contempt, was a catalyst for others. Quite energetic, she was ceaselessly active and her work produced real adventures. The book retains some of this excitement. Colorful events and interesting episodes dot the pages.

Goldman's avowed candor in recording some events also adds interest. She does not flinch from describing her sexual feelings nor her embarrassments. For example, she reports Reitman's unreliabilities and her complex attraction to him despite her distaste for his weaknesses. Her naive, abortive attempt at prostitution to gain funds for the assassination of Frick is depicted in amusing detail. Such explicitness, which was undoubtedly titillating when the work was published, is still appealing. But this appearance of openness is somewhat misleading. As Candace Falk notes in *Love, Anarchy, and Emma Goldman,* the scope of the work, ranging from 1869 to 1928 and covering literally scores of people and events, "gave it the illusion of holding back on nothing."[19] Falk's discussion, however, reveals how Goldman deliberately concealed details of her tumultuous relationship with Reitman, perhaps because her personal emotional life contradicted her public analyses of love. Often, Goldman did not confide her feelings fully, preferring to offer "high-minded" and even smug analyses of her emotional reactions. For example, her descriptions of the ends of her love affairs typically attributed their termination to her dedication to the anarchist cause and to the sacrifices necessary for individuals like herself who were fully committed to an ideal.[20]

Her candor leads her to reveal both her strengths and weaknesses. She details episodes that indicate her dogmatism, aggressiveness, and insensitivity. Her forcefulness and abrasiveness are abundantly apparent, although she seems to regard these as virtues. Sometimes, her description of her virtues is self-serving. One modern critic notes that in contrast to the autobiographies of many women, Goldman's "demonstrates no difficulty in self-assertion; on the contrary, self-glorification, often explicit, dominates it."[21] Although Goldman could be a passionate, loyal, and sympathetic friend, her tendency to point this out about herself and to minimize the virtues of others is amusing rather than totally convincing. As Wexler notes in discussing the difficulties in separating truth from fiction in relation to Goldman, she developed "her own myth of herself as earth mother and as tragic heroine, which she dramatized in her massive autobiography."[22] Her vanity and self-delusion do not obscure her real virtues, however. Events reveal Goldman as courageous, forthright, loyal, energetic, and unusually honest. What emerges is a portrait of a confident, assertive, and committed individual who both loved and hated with vehemence.

With all its exciting events and apparent candor, however, *Living My Life* has other substantial flaws. In focusing too narrowly on the details of some experiences, Goldman obscures some significant developments. Reporting her reactions to all the characters and including insignificant particulars sometimes produces a tedious account of even trivial occurrences, as when she catalogs the cause and course of a fellow prisoner's illness (670). Although the episode builds her case against the brutality in prisons, it is disproportionally circumstantial. The larger point is obscured in the plethora of detail. As Freda Kirchwey points out in her review for the *Nation,* the book is unnecessarily full and detailed.[23] Because of Goldman's penchant for detail and variety of activities, the reader has difficulty keeping track of individual characters and causes that appear and disappear in the complex story. Charles A. Madison in *Critics and Crusaders* notes that "her unrepressed egotism prompts her to relate personal incidents which have little bearing on her own development and none on that of anarchism—incidents that sometimes reveal petty malice and that might better have been left unrecorded."[24] In short, by providing too much detail indiscriminately, the autobiography often sacrifices clarity and focus.

Goldman's chronology in the book is also problematic. Her emphasis on chronology after the initial chapters makes it hard to perceive the development of any single aspect of her activities or personality. In contrast, her disconnected recital of her childhood experiences, sprinkled throughout the early chapters, obscures a coherent picture of her girlhood and the factors at work in her development. Interestingly, both these flaws stem from the same source: Goldman's focus on herself as an anarchist. This focus leads her to use a flashback technique in discussing her childhood, keeping her arrival in New York as a starting point, and to trace the development of important events as they occurred. In typical fashion, Goldman answers a criticism of her chronology by noting that "life, itself, is a crazy quilt and so must be the record of life." Citing modern psychologists, she argues that her technique was a modern approach and objections to it "rather old-fashioned."[25] Still, despite her reasoning, the book's chronological conflations are troublesome.

Goldman's focus on the history of her cause also eclipses her concern for the people she encounters. She provides few interesting insights into the personalities or the relationships she chronicles. Despite her long friendships with Alexander Berkman, Max Baginski, Harry Weinberger, and her devotion to her niece Stella Cominsky, the reader gets little sense of them as distinctive or real people. Goldman records her father's early brutalities to her and later describes her changed attitude toward him, but explains her altered view solely in terms of her ideological perception of her father as an example of society's debasement of human beings (447–48). In essence, her concentration on the events in her career as an agitator and on the anarchist movement overshadows the people in her autobiography. In her own life story, as in her analysis of drama, individual characterization is subservient to her anarchism.

In a more telling omission, Goldman fails to probe her own motivations and personality. Falk traces this lack of insight to Goldman's inability to recognize her own faults and to her tendency to repress and redirect her feelings of pain and anger.[26] Undoubtedly Goldman was also somewhat self-deluded. One explanation may lie in her strong aversion to religious morality and its notions of sin and guilt. Although she was a highly moral person, Goldman had no tolerance for such religious constraints and her determination to live freely and to develop fully may have made her hesitant to appraise her actions and motivations critically. Her metaphor of "unrestrained growth" that underlay her anarchist ideology also probably disinclined her from critical self-analysis. For whatever reasons, Goldman tended to record events and her role in them without evaluating her own motivations and attitudes.

A closely related weakness in the work is pointed out by Ordway Tead in the *Yale Review* and by Waldo Frank in the *New Republic*: her failure to explain the ideology that motivated her. Tead comments, "This portrait . . . cannot fail to be compelling and stirring. Yet I wish the picture might have included something of her distinctly intellectual outlook. There is a sense in which the book, personal though it is, is too objective and not sufficiently reflective. One sees an eager rebel against all personal restraints; but one searches in some bewilderment both for the secret of her impassioned life-long and sacrificial devotion, and for the ideas which were to her 'The Cause.' "[27] Admitting that Goldman was a "deep, hearty presence" in her autobiography, Frank notes, "She is never the analyst or integrator of her story. . . . In a life so purely dynamic, there is no pause for thought, hence her book's total lack of ideology."[28] The book is a record of life, rather than a reflection on it. Though it focuses on the anarchist movement, the reader gets little coherent sense of the ideology itself. Even Goldman's descriptions of the conflict between her feelings in her complicated sexual relationships and her political commitments do not convey the sources of her values nor the bases of her choices. Goldman relates the events in which she was involved, but does not convey the factors that drew her so forcefully into the roles she played.

The financial returns of the book were very disappointing. Although the two-volume work published by Knopf at $7.50 apparently did well in libraries and sold relatively well in some areas, Goldman received very little from it. She wrote to her longtime friend Percival Gerson that although the reviews were good "the sale is nil. . . . My publisher has certainly made a blunder, by no means the only one, but there is nothing I can do to change matters, except to hope that he might put out a cheaper edition in the not-too-distant future. I have depended on the returns from my book, not to make me rich, but to secure me for a while. The disappointment is doubly bitter."[29] But no other edition materialized. In fact, when Alfred A. Knopf was asked to support Goldman's return to the United States for lectures both by serving on a sponsoring committee and by making a contribution, he agreed to serve, but added: "I do not, however, feel justified in making any financial contribution to the cause at this time as Miss Goldman's *Autobiography* still shows me a loss of several thousand dollars, representing money that I advanced to her in connection with it and which the book has not yet earned."[30]

Although *Living My Life* did not garner funds for Goldman, it received many favorable reviews. R. A. Preston, professor of English literature at Columbia, who reviewed the manuscript for Knopf prior to publication, was enthusiastic:

The book itself, it seems to me, can hardly escape being called a masterpiece. Rousseau's *Confessions* are poverty-stricken in incident and pallid in rhetoric beside this enthusiastic vitality. When Bernard Shaw said, long ago, that there could never be a true biography, because no man was good enough to tell the whole truth about himself or bad enough to tell it about someone else . . . he cannot have known Emma Goldman. So far as is humanly possible this strikes me as a complete revelation of one of the most vivid and genuinely vital lives and personalities of our time.[31]

Many contemporary reviewers seconded his opinion. The *New York Times* reviewer judged it to be "a human document of the most absorbing interest. . . . Another writer telling the same incidents might easily have made them dull, absurd, or indecent, but as Miss Goldman tells them they contain no trace of dullness, absurdity or indecency. . . . She belongs to a species which is at least temporarily vanishing and she is in her own right something which is rarely found . . . an original and picturesque personality. . . . Her autobiography is one of the great books of its kind."[32] Even reviewers like those at *Time* and the *New Republic,* who saw anarchism as passé and her efforts as misguided, were impressed by her energy and integrity.[33]

Later reviewers have also found the book impressive. Charles A. Madison writes: "It is a lively story, palpitating with strong feeling and epitomizing the blazing years of her anarchist activity. The writing is vivacious, forceful, exciting. The narrative is colorful and wholly uninhibited. Emma's strong personality stamps every page."[34] Feminist critic Patricia Meyer Spacks, who accuses Goldman of exaggerating and overdramatizing her emotions (a charge her contemporaries also made), still admires her candor and self-assertiveness.[35] Perhaps Richard Drinnon's assessment is most apt: "Her *Autobiography* was a work of art primarily because to a large extent her life was as well."[36]

Chapter Six

Goldman as a Rhetor

All that can be done is to plant the seeds of thought.
—Anarchism and Other Essays

Goldman's Development as a Rhetor

Although Goldman wrote extensively, she remained primarily a speaker, both in natural aptitude and public effectiveness. As Berkman noted, "E.'s forte is the platform, not the pen, as she herself knows very well."[1] Despite her initial skepticism about her own speaking abilities, Goldman appreciated the influence of oratory and the importance of effective delivery. Deeply moved by the speeches of Johann Most and Johanna Greie on the Haymarket tragedy, she particularly savored their earnest, intense delivery.[2] From Goldman's purview, speaking was an important endeavor, capable of exciting high passion and changing lives. Success in that art, she recognized, entailed dynamic delivery.

Despite her enthusiasm for public speaking, becoming an orator was not easy for Goldman. Her initial stage fright even before the brief talks that Most encouraged her to make at meetings was almost overwhelming. "I would experience a kind of sinking sensation the moment I got up on to my feet, I would feel faint. Desperately I would grip the chair in front of me, my heart throbbing, my knees trembling—everything in the hall would turn hazy. Then I would become aware of my voice, far, far away, and finally I would sink back in my seat in a cold sweat." Apparently this inner turmoil did not impede her communication because, although she felt her talks were "incoherent," Berkman remarked on her "calm and self-control."[3]

Her first independent lecture tour, organized by Most, taught her a valuable lesson. Although Goldman could already stir audiences with her vigorous delivery, she had to express her own ideas instead of relying on others to provide her with substance. There-

after, she spent long hours reading and researching to prepare herself
to speak with both knowledge and conviction. Long after Goldman
developed her delivery skills, she retained the habit of meticulous
preparation set in these early days. The frequent, direct references
to diverse sources and the allusions in her essays reveal the scope of
her lecture research.

Throughout her career, Goldman's speaking provided the stimulus for her writing. Because she lectured frequently on the same
topics, polishing her presentations each time, her careful notes provided an excellent basis for essays. Pressures of time, her own hectic
schedule, and her editorial control at *Mother Earth* suggest that many
lectures were published as essays with few changes. A comparison
of her few extant lecture notes, which have never been published,
and her essays reveals no substantial stylistic differences, except frequent misspellings. Thus, Goldman's writing was an organic outgrowth of her speaking.

Yet despite her speaking skills, after years on the platform, she
realized the limitations of oratory and saw writing as a more effective
tool for social change. In *Anarchism and Other Essays* she traces her
early enthusiasm for oratory and then admits: "Gradually, and with
no small struggle against this realization, I came to see that oral
propaganda is at best a measure of shaking people from their leth-
argy: it leaves no lasting impression." She felt oratory attracted
those seeking entertainment, and the speaker had to contend with
the crowd's restlessness, "distracted by a thousand non-essentials."[4]
Books offered a more intimate relationship between writer and reader,
allowing the reader to find what he or she was actively seeking.
Despite her admiration for the spoken word, Goldman finally preferred written communication because, although it reached fewer
people, it allowed her "to reach the few who really want to learn
rather than the many who come to be amused."[5]

In considering Emma Goldman as a rhetor, it is important to
remember that she was primarily an agitator whose natural forum
was the lecture platform. Many features of her rhetoric, especially
the flaws in her reasoning and her frequently awkward and melodramatic style, would be less objectionable to a live audience caught
up in her dynamic delivery than to an armchair reader. Moreover,
some elements, like her sarcasm, were most effective in stimulating
interest and reactions in listeners, although they often can be un-
suitable and abrasive to a reader. Because Goldman's aim as a speaker

was to stimulate and agitate her listeners, her rhetoric was probably well suited to her objective. But the very rhetorical features that were provocative to her listeners are those that are less successful to her readers, who are removed from the direct impact of her strong personality.

Rhetorical Persona and Tone

In all her works, Goldman sees herself as an enlightened observer whose mission is to instruct others. She consistently suggests that she is the objective commentator, analyzing and explaining events for the less perspicacious. Her perceptions are "indisputable fact," her intention is "to elucidate what Anarchism really stands for" or to expose the "superstitions" surrounding love and marriage, and she can "dissect" the "modern fetich" of suffrage.[6] Goldman's persona is that of one able to see the issues more clearly than others and to set them before an audience with coolheaded reason.

This perception of herself and her mission causes her tone to be didactic and often dogmatic. Although all her essays convey this, the introduction to "Marriage and Love" is an especially clear illustration: "The popular notion about marriage and love is that they are synonymous, that they spring from the same motives, and cover the same human needs. Like most popular notions this also rests not on actual facts, but on superstition. Marriage and love have nothing in common; they are as far apart as the poles; are, in fact, antagonistic to each other."[7] The imperiously didactic tone of her essays is also clear in her frequent references to "all intelligent observers," "advanced criminologists," "thinking men and women the world over," "modern writers," and "the most advanced students" to support her views.[8] She and they are the intellectual vanguard, pointing out the road to enlightenment and social revolution.

This deliberate didacticism shades into a dogmatic and authoritarian rhetorical stance at odds with her anarchistic ideals. Goldman's judgments of institutions, attitudes, and practices are so absolute that they brook no alternative perspective. The essays on suffrage, woman's emancipation, patriotism, and political violence provide excellent examples of her dogmatic analysis. She also often prescribes behavior for her readers in a most unanarchistic fashion. For example, her general indictment of suffrage makes participation in elections not just meaningless but the activity of a dupe or fool. Although Goldman ostensibly refuses to offer concrete proposals for many social problems like conscription, for example, her strongly expressed antipathy for certain behaviors is, in effect, a dictum for personal activities.

Goldman's self-confidence and dogmatism also make her disdainful toward the public and toward other viewpoints. In her zeal to expose the abuses of society, she frequently paints a picture of the public that is at best insulting. Even when she puts herself among the group she is criticizing, her rhetorical stance makes her superiority clear. For example, in exposing the fallacies of patriotism, Goldman writes:

We Americans claim to be a peace-loving people. We hate bloodshed; we are opposed to violence. Yet we go into spasms of joy over the possibility of projecting dynamite bombs from flying machines upon helpless citizens. We are ready to hang, electrocute, or lynch anyone, who, from economic necessity will risk his own life in an attempt upon that of some industrial magnate. Yet our hearts swell with pride at the thought that America is becoming the most powerful nation on earth, and that it will eventually plant her iron foot on the necks of all other nations. Such is the logic of patriotism.[9]

Goldman's disdain toward other views is also clear in her frequent use of epithets like "absurd," "outrageous," "ridiculous," and "folly" to describe them. Goldman was conscious of her attitude, for in the preface to *Anarchism and Other Essays* she reacts in advance to an objection she feels will be raised about her stance. The passage reflects her rhetorical persona accurately: "No doubt, I shall be excommunicated as an enemy of the people, because I repudiate the mass as a creative factor. I shall prefer that rather than be guilty of the demagogic platitudes so commonly in vogue as a bait for the people. I realize the malady of the oppressed and disinherited masses only too well, but I refuse to prescribe the usual ridiculous palliatives."[10]

Frequently, Goldman's disdain produces biting sarcasm. Of the contention of intellectuals that they are engaged in enlightening the public, she writes harshly: "What are they doing to cut loose from their chains, and how dare they boast that they are helping the masses? Yet you know that they are engaged in uplift work. What a farce! They, also pitiful and low in their slavery, so dependent and helpless."[11] She labels the American woman's suffrage movement "a parlor affair, absolutely detached from the economic needs of the people."[12] Christ's preaching is "a sentimental mysticism, obscure and confused ideals lacking originality and vitality."[13] Refuting the ideal of the emancipated woman as depicted in a contemporary novel, Goldman deplores the emotional coldness of this model by sympathizing with the woman's would-be lover: "I fear if they had formed a union, the young man would have risked freezing to death."[14] In another essay she characterizes marriage succinctly as "that poor little State and Church-begotten weed."[15] This tendency toward sarcasm is even more pronounced in the columns in *Mother Earth* that reported her travels. Sometimes sarcasm and ridicule shape longer passages. Her caustic refutation of the Beatitudes, which runs about 650 words, is a case in point. An excerpt suggests the intensity and flavor of her attack:

"Blessed are the poor in spirit, for theirs is the Kingdom of Heaven." Heaven must be an awfully dull place if the poor in spirit live there. How can anything creative, anything vital, useful and beautiful come from the poor in spirit? "Blessed are the meek, for they shall inherit the earth." What a preposterous notion! What incentive to slavery, inactivity, and parasitism! Besides, it is not true that the meek can inherit anything. Just because humanity has been meek, the earth has been stolen from it.[16]

If Goldman's sarcasm was effective in rousing her lethargic listeners or baiting those who came to heckle, she sometimes used it ill-advisedly so that it worked against her best interests. Perhaps the clearest case was her final plea to the jury in her 1917 trial. Even if we admit that the proceedings had been biased against her, her opening words to the jury can only have polarized them still further and confirmed their view of her. She sarcastically describes the actions of the United States marshal who came to arrest "the big fish" of the no-conscription campaign. After dashing upstairs, prepared "to stake their lives for their country, . . . his hosts of heroic warriors, . . . sensational enough to satisfy the famous circus men, Barnum and Bailey, [discovered] the two dangerous disturbers and trouble-makers . . . wielding not a sword, nor a gun or a bomb, but merely their pens! Verily, it required courage to catch such big fish." She goes on to characterize these actions metaphorically as the first act of a farce that concludes with their transporting "the villains in a madly dashing automobile—which broke every traffic regulation and barely escaped crushing everyone in its way." The third act is the court proceedings, which because of the government's failure to equip itself with "better dramatic material to sustain the continuity of the play . . . fell flat, utterly, and presents the question, Why such a tempest in a teapot?"[17] Although clever and undoubtedly amusing to her sympathizers, this description can only have intensified the jury's hostility to her and made them less receptive to her later defense of anarchism as a constructive force.

Goldman's sarcasm gives a sharp edge to many passages and even to entire essays, and its sources seem to be a compelling earnestness and concern. She is stern and even harsh because she sees the destructiveness and invidiousness of many social practices. Goldman argues always from a commitment to principles to which she adheres with integrity and fervor. Moreover, her deep concern sometimes produces an empathetic depiction of human beings, as in her essays on Ferrer and political violence, which works as a counterweight to her vitriol. Thus, Goldman's honesty and deep concern sometimes help counteract her supercilious and caustic tone.

In essence, Goldman's perception of her role and her strong ideological bias give her essays a didactic and dogmatic tone. Her disdain toward the public and her sarcasm create a rather intimidating rhetorical persona. Although her integrity and concern provide some relief from her impatience with and intolerance of other views, Goldman emerges in her works as a provocative, rather than appealing, rhetor. This persona may generate respect in the reader, but rarely affection. Consequently, and ironically, her rhetorical tone probably produced the stimulation she sought in her audiences at the expense of her personal persuasiveness.

Organization and Development of Ideas

Because Goldman's goal is didactic and because she values reason, the organization of her texts is straightforward and unambiguous. Each contains a brief, direct introductory passage, a clearly developed body, which explicates or provides evidence for an explicit thesis, and a short, usually emotionally charged conclusion, which frequently contains strong inspirational appeals.

While her lectures sometimes began with a brief reference to the situation, Goldman's essays address the topic at hand immediately, with few efforts at graceful or indirect approaches to the issues. Occasionally, Goldman begins with quoted material or rhetorical questions. [18] More frequently she begins with direct statements that establish the direction of her argument: "If I were to give a summary of the tendency of our times, I would say, Quantity. The multitude, the mass spirit, dominates everywhere, destroying quality." [19] Sometimes she uses these direct statements to shock her audience. Her essay on love and marriage, for example, announces that the two notions are not synonymous, but instead antagonistic. [20] In her essay on woman's suffrage, Goldman immediately assaults the audience's conception of themselves as progressive thinkers: "We boast of the age of advancement, of science, and progress. Is it not strange, then, that we still belive in fetich worship." [21] The "fetich" is universal suffrage.

In reading Goldman's essays, we are struck by how seldom she attempts to mollify her listeners and establish common ground with them. Her tendency toward confrontation rather than conciliation often undercuts her impact, particularly when she insults her audience early in the essay or speech. Goldman's address to the jury, cited previously, is a clear case. Another example occurs in "Minorities versus Majorities," in which Goldman labels quantity the "tendency of our time. . . . Our entire life—production, politics, and education—rests on quantity, on numbers. The worker who once took pride in the thoroughness and quality of his work, has been replaced by brainless, incompetent automatons." [22] Although the use of "our" creates a sense of common concern, and although some audiences could easily identify with the anonymity and impersonality that she depicts in the work environment, the phrase "incompetent automatons" is hardly flattering to the workers she hoped to persuade. Goldman's failure to build common ground with her listeners and readers in her introductions probably limited her rhetorical effectiveness when she was not preaching to the already converted. The brevity and clear focus of her introductions highlight her thesis effectively, however.

The internal structure of Goldman's essays varies, but all are clearly organized and developed. The major essays fall into two broad categories in terms of organization: (1) those that use an expository pattern to explicate her social and political philosophies and (2) those that explore the causes of current problems or examine the effect of particular attitudes, proposals, and institutions.

The first group, which includes her essays on anarchism, the modern school, and drama, uses a simple expository format. For example, the essay on anarchism first defines it explicitly, then explains how it counteracts the contemporary emphasis on society's domination over the individual, and finally details how property, religion, and the state all repress the individual. Some essays in this group are less explicit in their organization, but their development of Goldman's views is always systematic and easy to follow. Only the essay on "Francisco Ferrer and the Modern School" seems poorly organized because it both reacts to his "martyrdom" and explains the modern school movement, two loosely related topics.

The second group, which includes all other essays on disparate topics, either seeks the sources of the contemporary problems Goldman perceives or probes the impact of social institutions or individuals. In analyzing the causes of a problem, Goldman often substantiates its existence initially by citing statistics (on the rising crime rate, the costs of prisons, or the rising divorce rate, for example) or by referring to authorities like Friedrich Nietzsche or Max Stirner for confirmation. In every case, she then advances a clear thesis about the reasons for the problem, supporting her analysis with explanations, historical illustrations, and reasoning. For example, "The Traffic in Women" suggests that low pay, wretched working conditions, sexual repression, the double standard, and societal stereotypes of women are all direct causes of prostitution. In her essays on morality, patriotism, preparedness, education, emancipation, and puritanism, Goldman concentrates on explicating the impact of institutions and policies on individuals. In "Victims of Morality," she argues that American sexual morality can lead women to only one of three alternatives, all undesirable, while in "Patriotism," Goldman traces its inimical effect on individual people, on society, on soldiers, and on the cause of the worker. Although Goldman's essays vary in internal organization, each nonetheless provides a clear development of an explicit thesis. Clear reasoning, examples, statistics, explanations, and quotations help substantiate her views.

Her address to the jury reveals a slightly different pattern that demonstrates her intuitive sense of how to organize material effectively. After her biting introduction, Goldman reviews the evidence and arguments against her, using reasoning and frequent rhetorical questions to refute them. For example, the prosecution had apparently called a reporter who testified that Goldman had offered him material that encouraged resistance to the draft. Goldman effectively undercuts his testimony by drawing on the jury's own observation of the man: "Did any one of you receive the impression that the man was of conscriptable age, and if not, in what possible way is the giving of *Mother Earth* to a reporter for news purposes proof demonstrating the overt act?"[23] After refuting other charges, she defends her activities by describing them as part of human progress that must always operate outside the law, and then offers an eloquent reaffirmation of her anarchist beliefs and her faith in their ultimate triumph.

Like her introductions, Goldman's conclusions are brief, but rely much more typically on strong emotional appeals and inspirational declarations. At times she provides a sketchy solution to the problem that she has analyzed, or she offers a general direction for action. Other essays conclude with a vision of the future to inspire her readers. For example, her bleak analysis in "The Victims of Morality" ends on a sanguine note: "Morality has no terror for her who has risen beyond good and evil. And though morality may continue to devour its victims, it is utterly powerless in the face of the modern spirit, that shines in all its glory upon the brow of man and woman, liberated and unafraid."[24] Other essays are equally emotional, but usually less rosy. Her essay on Ferrer asserts: "The consciousness that his executioners represent a dying age, and that his was the living truth, sustained him in the last heroic moments. 'A dying age and a living truth, the living burying the dead.' "[25]

Goldman eschews summaries or reviews, except very brief ones, to carry her readers on to such emotionally charged endings. Unlike her introductions, which sometimes contain sarcasm or vitriolic charges, the endings of Goldman's essays employ strong, emotional appeals devoid of irony. New dawns, light, rising tides, and scaled mountains are frequent commonplace metaphors that give her essays dramatic closure.

Use of Reasoning and Refutation

Within her essays, Goldman relied heavily on reasoning and evidence to develop her ideas. Although one may disagree with her interpretations and question some of her evidence, the essays usually follow an orderly movement from data to conclusion. For example, in "The Failure of Christianity," Goldman claims that Christianity's flaws are inherent in its doctrine, not in its institutionalization. She cites the Beatitudes as evidence of Christianity's encouragement of docility in the face of problems. Because Christianity supports such passivity, she concludes that anyone concerned with changing society must repudiate it.[26] In other essays, Emma uses quotations and factual material to support her claims. She cites the increased military expenses of various nations to substantiate her contention that patriotism is costly, and she presents the details of the Homestead strike to demonstrate how institutionalized forces provoke reactive violence.[27] Her essays are sprinkled with references to other authorities (many unfortunately unfamiliar to her audience) to substantiate her assertions. In essence, Goldman's writing gains rhetorical force because of her extensive use of clear reasoning, varied evidence, and appeals to authority.

In some cases her reasoning is conspicuously flawed, however. Her argument against woman's suffrage as necessarily introducing more intolerance and Puritanism into political affairs is weak and inconsistent. She uses scanty evidence of specific laws in Idaho, Colorado, Wyoming, and Utah, which had woman's suffrage, to support her claims. We can question the typicality of her examples as well as her consistency: she had earlier noted that the undesirable situation in Australia, where women were enfranchised, could not be traced solely to the impact of women's right to vote.[28] Although both pieces of data confirm her view that woman's suffrage did not resolve pressing social problems, the conflict between her statement that women's votes will create intolerant laws and her admission that they have had little real effect in other places is obvious.

Another notable and prevalent weakness in Goldman's reasoning is her tendency to overgeneralize and to argue from prejudice. Her indictment of the church's involvement in prostitution reveals these practices. She refers only to one case of a church's real estate holdings to prove her broad claim. Moreover, she conflates quite disparate theologies and social mores into a monolithic "religion," which she avers, has always fostered prostitution and hailed it as a virtue.[29] Her apologia for political violence, her analysis of criminality, and her analysis of marriage as destructive of love reveal this same tendency to overgeneralize on the basis of highly selective cases.

Goldman's lapses in reasoning, however, should not obscure the accuracy and insight of many of her arguments. Her predictions about the emotional and psychological repercussions of women's emancipation accord closely with the subsequent experiences of many women and her criticisms of prison employment parallel many experts' analyses. Undoubtedly, many of her assessments are not original, but her systematic and clear explanations of causal relationships probably enlightened her audience.

Goldman also frequently developed her viewpoint by refuting attitudes or arguments proposed by her opponents. Although her techniques varied with issues and contexts, her rebuttal skills were usually keen. Sometimes she disposed of opposing arguments with dispatch, a few sentences serving her purpose; other times an entire essay was an extended refutation of a viewpoint. In each case, her clear, systematic organization enhanced her rebuttal.

One of her frequent rebuttal techniques was the relabeling or the reinterpretation of concepts to establish or refute their desirability. For example, to demonstrate that marriage and love are contradictory concepts, Goldman highlights the crassness and parasitism marriage encourages in women, contrasting it with the idealism and independence flowing from free love. Using "name-calling," a standard propaganda device, she redefines the stereotypical division of labor between men as providers and women as homemakers, calling it "paternalism" and "parasitism."[30] This same relabeling as refutation occurs in her essays on patriotism and on minorities versus majorities, among others. Her final speech to the jury in her 1917 trial provides a beautiful example of Goldman's skill with this technique. Noting that her activities had been castigated as being "outside the law," she educes examples from American history (the revolutionary heroes), from religious realms (Jesus), and from the French Revolution to support her claim that progress also grows from activities initially outside the established legal framework. Goldman finally compares the law to "a chariot wheel which grinds all alike without regard to time, place, and condition. Progress knows nothing of fixity. . . . Progress is ever renewing, ever becoming, ever changing—*never is it within the law*.[31] In essence, she transforms the charge of "being outside the law" into an indication of progressive thought, a central American virtue.

Goldman is also quite skillful in answering specific charges and in arguing from probability. In her essay on Ferrer, for example, she adroitly refutes the claims that he participated in an antimilitary uprising. She first notes that the initial indictment made no mention of such participation, inferring that the charge was developed to stop Ferrer's antireligious activities rather than to identify his real involvements. Next, she attacks the evidence used against him, especially the witnesses whom he was never allowed to confront. Finally, she argues that his psychology made it impossible for him to have been involved, because he was reputedly a good organizer and planner and would not, therefore, have been associated with a spontaneous, unorganized uprising. She continues her arguments in this vein, constructing a tight defense of Ferrer both by examining the facts of the proceedings and by appealing to probabilities in light of his character.

One of her most frequent rebuttal strategies is her use of the ad hominem argument, both against specific people and groups. With individuals she discredits their motivations as well as their intelligence and ability. In "The Hypocrisy of Puritanism," she assaults Anthony Comstock, a well-known vice fighter and a longtime personal enemy: "Art, literature, the drama, the privacy of the mails, in fact, our most intimate tastes, are at the mercy of this inexorable tyrant. Anthony Comstock, or some equally ignorant policeman, has been given the power to desecrate genius, to soil and mutilate the sublimest creation of nature—the human form." In other passages, Goldman terms him "the auto-crat of American morals," who "like a thief in the night . . . sneaks into the private lives of people," putting to shame "the infamous Third Division of the Russian secret police."[32] Of Woodrow Wilson and Theodore Roosevelt, both capitalistic warmongers in her view, she writes: "The difference between Wilson and Roosevelt is this: Roosevelt, a born bully, uses the club; Wilson, the historian, the college professor, wears the smooth, polished university mask, but underneath it, he, like Roosevelt, has but one aim, to serve the big interests, to add to those who are growing phenomenally rich by the manufacture of military supplies."[33] No group receives more severe treatment at Goldman's hands than churchmen. "Jesuitical" is a favorite word to describe coldhearted manipulativeness. She labels the clergy "leeches," their doctrines "poisonous weeds," and the church "a black monster."[34] The depiction of the law enforcement officers involved in her arrest in 1917 as Keystone Cop–like figures is a further case of her use of this technique.[35]

Clearly, Goldman recognized the necessity of reasoning with her audience and, if possible, refuting many of their preconceptions to prepare them for her new views. Moreover, it seemed to her that anarchism was the only rational ideology. Her refutation strategies were a crucial part of her efforts to awaken and stimulate her audience's thinking; and although not perfectly executed, her rebuttals did provoke thought and invite reaction.

Style

According to all accounts, Goldman was very effective as a lecturer, but her style is less successful in print. Although her works are still enjoyable to read, they lack the polish and grace characteristic of the greatest essays. One critic, noting that her printed works lack the "dynamic appeal" of her lectures, labels them "the work of a forceful agitator: clear, pointed, spirited, but without originality or intellectual rigor."[36] This assessment highlights the key strength of Goldman's style—its clarity and vividness—and accurately suggests its limitations.

Although Goldman loved literature, she deplored art for art's sake. In some respects, thus, her style is unstudied; she trusted spontaneity over premeditated art. She wrote to one correspondent who had criticized the simple style of her autobiography: "One's style is one's personality, the moment one begins to write according to a pattern one is bound to be stifled."[37] Consequently, she sought to communicate her ideas clearly and directly, perhaps relying on the ideas themselves to excite her listeners. A review of *Anarchism and Other Essays* in the *Baltimore Evening Sun* indicates that she was successful in this: "Every child who can read can easily understand and digest every word of this wonderful exposure of all the crimes of capitalism."[38] But while her autobiography has a straightforward, even dull style, her essays are more colorful, reflecting her fiery personality more accurately.

The liveliness in Goldman's essays stems primarily from her colorful language and sometimes effective images. She is particularly energetic with epithets and metaphoric depictions. The opening of "The Failure of Christianity," for example, refers to "the counterfeiters and poisoners of ideas in their attempt to obscure the line between truth and falsehood."[39] Militarism is a "bloody spectre," the state "an altar of political freedom maintained for the purpose of human sacrifice," and individuals with "fat political jobs" are "parasites who stalk about the world."[40] Property recognizes its own "gluttonous appetite for greater wealth" and the "public palate is like a dumping ground; it relishes anything that needs no mental mastication."[41] In a passage from her essay "Was My Life Worth Living?" she reaffirms her objections to all forms of government by reiterating her belief that states always oppress individuals; the cases in which states do not are "as rare as roses growing on icebergs."[42] This vivid image cements her notion in the reader's mind.

Neither subtle nor original, Goldman relied heavily on standard images, adapting them to her particular topics. Three groups of images recur most frequently: light versus dark, enslavement versus punishment, and life versus death. Despite her use of these commonplace, even trite images, her heavy irony and unrestrained vitriol help to invigorate them. In attacking suffrage, she uses a commonplace revolutionary image of the proletariat in chains, but enlivens it with concrete depiction, irony, and sarcasm: "The poor, stupid, free American citizen! Free to starve, free to tramp the highways of this great country, he enjoys universal suffrage, and by that right, he has forged chains about his limbs."[43] Not surprisingly, Goldman is most successful when her metaphors reflect her pungent personality. Her positive images (of anarchism as a new dawn, for example) tend to be both trite and maudlin.

Although Goldman's language and images are often colorful and effective, her syntax is less remarkable. Rhetorical questions, parallelism, and antithesis are common features. The results are as often awkward as effective. Few passages are memorable for their stylistic polish and verve. An excerpt from her essay "Minorities versus Majorities" reflects the weaknesses and strengths characteristic of her syntax.

Not because I do not feel with the oppressed, the disinherited of the earth; not because I do not know the shame, the horror, the indignity of the lives the people lead, do I repudiate the majority as a creative force for the good. Oh, no, no! But because I know so well that as a compact mass it has never stood for justice or equality. It has suppressed the human voice, subdued the human spirit, chained the human body. As a mass its aim has always been to make life uniform, gray and monotonous as the desert. As a mass it will always be the annihilator of individuality, of free initiative, of originality.[44]

Although several ways to improve the passage are obvious, the rather skillful repetition and parallelism help compensate for the awkward syntax ("Do I repudiate"). As this excerpt reveals, Goldman often packs her parallel structures too densely together and uses too many compound elements. The result is a heavy, even turgid style.

In sum, Goldman's prose style, although usually clear and vivid, is also heavy and graceless. Strained syntax and a tendency toward wordiness, particularly in passages using repetition, rob her written rhetoric of life and force. At times her vivid language and her colorful imagery leaven her turgid style, but her essays generally lack the vitality that she must have conveyed as a speaker.

Goldman's Delivery

Although no films or records of Goldman's speaking exist, numerous contemporary reports attest to her effectiveness as an orator. Even the judge and prosecuting district attorney in her 1917 trial commented on her eloquence. Evidence suggests that Goldman was an energetic, sincere, and flamboyant speaker who apparently used few notes. These features, coupled with her rather surprising appearance, explain much of her effectiveness.

Goldman's matronly appearance probably often disarmed her audience, which knew her colorful reputation. Short and stocky from youth, she came increasingly to resemble a plump peasant grandmother. A columnist for the *Nation* in 1917 described her as "a small, wiry woman, about fifty years old, who might be passed anywhere in a crowd without notice."[45] The wiriness undoubtedly referred to Goldman's agility, for pictures of the time reveal her undeniable plumpness. One observer noted that she had "a stocky figure like a peasant woman, a face of fierce strength like a female pugilist."[46] Her appearance coupled with her energy probably surprised the naive observer, for she did not look the part of a rabble-rouser or an advocate of free love. One 1939 observer remarked that "the first impression she conveys, on introduction, is a trifle disappointing." But he added: "E. G. is a human dynamo if there ever was one."[47]

Because of her appearance, Goldman's energetic delivery was all the more startling. One indication of her energy was her rapid-fire, forceful delivery. Reporting on the trial for conspiracy, Berkman noted that her two-hundred-word-a-minute pace made her the third fastest speaker in the country and a stenographer testified that her very rapid rate made transcription very difficult.[48] A report of the

trial in the *New York Herald Tribune* observed that even in the
courtroom she used a "Voice Still Pitched for Crowds."[49]

Her intensity and sincerity enlivened her delivery. Roger Baldwin
reported: "I heard E. G. speak many times, always without notes
or script, forcefully and persuasively whatever the audience. She
conveyed a direct and uncompromising quality which left no doubt
as to her feelings."[50] In her comments about the 1917 trial, Margaret
Anderson described Goldman as an "earnest preacher."[51] Hutchins
Hapgood, too, was struck by "the vigor and passion of her personality."[52] An earnestness, born out of her deep anarchist convictions
and sustained by her compassion for the victims of social injustice,
marked her delivery.

Goldman was also flamboyant as a speaker. She interacted energetically with her audience, often playing off of their initial hostility. Her standing on the stage with a handkerchief in her mouth
as a symbolic protest against being kept from speaking during the
legal proceedings around her 1917 trial suggests the kind of dramatic
gestures she enjoyed. A *New York Times* report of her "barn speech"
on Alden Freeman's New Jersey estate after she was barred from
speaking in New York City reveals clearly her dynamic interaction
with the crowd. She harangued her listeners: "You have been too
busy making money to do anything worthwhile." A bit later the
following exchange occurred: " 'Now I want to add one word,' she
looked at the chief—'we are protected here.' 'It's cause we know
you,' put in the chief. 'Not at all,' said Miss Goldman, amid laughter, 'for if you knew me you'd know I can take care of myself. I am
here to protect you against yourselves.' A great burst of laughter
came from the crowd and more cheers."[53] Goldman said herself that
audiences often came alive as she spoke, and she particularly relished
active exchanges during a question period.

This crowd reaction was due, in part, to her extemporaneous
delivery. Although she prepared carefully, she spoke independently
of her notes, reacting to the crowd and altering her text to suit the
situation. Comparison of the length of her essays with her known
rapid speaking rate and reports of the duration of her speeches
suggests that she elaborated extensively on her prepared texts, probably with additional examples or commonplaces. Because Goldman
lectured repeatedly on the same topic, her freedom from her manuscript is not surprising, despite the fact that her first arrest for

inciting to riot made her wary of departing too freely from her planned remarks.

Although her supporters' praise for her oratorical skills is predictable, even her antagonists shared their views. Samuel Eliot Morrison, who heard her at Oxford in the 1920s, wrote: "She was about the finest woman orator I have ever heard."[54] Hutchins Hapgood, who had little regard for her ideas, felt himself on one occasion caught up in her speaking, which he termed "a pure poem of feeling, springing spontaneously into form. It made me feel that this must have happened before with her, not only in cafe conversations with the faithful, but in her innumerable trips throughout the country."[55] One stenographer, testifying at her trial in 1917, called her the best speaker he had ever heard.[56]

In sum, Goldman was an energetic and dynamic speaker. Her deep commitment to anarchism gave her intensity and courage. Given to flamboyant strategies, both verbal and nonverbal, she goaded her audience into active involvement. Although she prepared carefully, she apparently spoke extemporaneously, altering her approach to fit the situation; and if she sometimes harangued her listeners, at other times she excited their imaginations and stimulated their thinking.

Conclusion: Goldman's Rhetorical Effectiveness

As a rhetor, Goldman was primarily a propagandist who hoped to produce social change by educating and stimulating her audience. Many features of her rhetoric are well-suited for this goal. Her dogmatism and sarcasm provoke interest and stimulate thought; her clear organization and reasoning promote understanding; and her vivid language enlivens her discussions. These elements, combined with her dynamic delivery, made her a very effective agitator. In addition, her colorful reputation undoubtedly attracted listeners. J. Edgar Hoover's assessment that she and Berkman were "two of the most dangerous anarchists in this country" and his prediction that her return to society in 1919 would "result in undue harm" reflect her reputation as an agitator.[57]

Many of these same features limited her influence on the broader public, however. Her bitterness and sarcasm, her haranguing of the audience, and her personal flamboyance made Goldman intriguing but also intimidating and even easy to dismiss. Together with her radical anarchist views, these rhetorical features accentuated her dissimilarities from most Americans. In her effort to be candid and stimulating, Goldman often polarized her audience. Those already sympathetic to her outlook found inspiration and excitement in her words; those less ideologically committed perceived her prejudices, her abrasiveness, and the weakness of her evidence and arguments.

To the reader distant from her in time, her essays are interesting but not persuasive. Although one may accept many of her observations and admire her insights, the essays are too ideologically limited and have too much harangue. Ironically, Emma Goldman, who valued reason and objectivity, emerges as too much the ideologue to be convincing.

Chapter Seven

An Assessment

The Individual Instinct is the thing of value in the world.
—"Anarchism: What It Really Stands For"

Alix Kates Schulman in her introduction to the second edition of selections from Goldman's writings notes the tremendous surge of interest in Goldman in recent years. Goldman has, she observes, "re-emerged from obscurity to become a veritable password of radical feminism."[1] In the same vein Karen Rosenberg, in reviewing four recent books about Goldman, including Schulman's, agrees that "one would be hard-pressed to find another woman of the past who enjoys her privileged status in contemporary America, who is emblazoned on as many tee-shirts and postcards." But, as Rosenberg indicates, Goldman "has grown into a cult rather than a historical figure."[2] Adopted as a role model by many feminists and admired by groups seeking broad social changes, Goldman has reappeared in American life as a symbol of conscientious, spirited opposition to societal pressures.

Assessing the significance of such a figure is difficult, for she has in some senses passed into myth. To recognize our own attitudes in her writings and to appreciate her sensitivity to important social problems may lead us to canonize her in a way that her anarchist beliefs would find repugnant. On the other hand, to dismiss her as merely a colorful personality because she failed to achieve many of the things she advocated would violate her insistence on the importance of the enlightened individual. Either interpretation seems unbalanced and unfair to the honesty quintessentially characteristic of Emma Goldman.

My goal, thus, is to evaluate her in a spirit she would have preferred: appreciating her creative contributions and acknowledging her limitations. Because the focus of this work has been on Goldman as a rhetorician, my assessment is in those terms. Her success in coping with the dynamics of her own life, her attempts to cope with the conflict between her ideology and her personal experiences have been ably and fully discussed in other literature. The question now is what to make of Goldman and her rhetorical efforts. Because, as Schulman and Rosenberg note, Goldman has achieved new recognition in recent years, we must consider her impact, first, in her own day, then, in the longer perspective.

As a speaker and writer, Goldman undoubtedly changed individual lives. Hutchins Hapgood in his autobiography suggests her impact. While he finds her ideas uninteresting, he acknowledges that "there were thousands of men and women all over the country who loved her. She performed a distinct service—that of removing despair from those who otherwise would be hopeless. Those who would otherwise regard themselves as outcasts, after hearing Emma, often felt a new hope and thought better about themselves."[3] Although Hapgood cites the case of a young prostitute to prove his point, other, more privileged persons felt her power. Margaret Anderson recalls her first impression, which lead to her defending Goldman in an early issue of the *Little Review*. "I heard Emma Goldman lecture and had just enough time to turn anarchist before the presses closed."[4] If Anderson's conversion was temporary, Roger Baldwin's proved more lasting. Baldwin, who later founded the American Civil Liberties Union, remembered going to hear her when he was a young man fresh out of Harvard. Despite his initial skepticism, he avers, "It was the eye-opener of my life. Never before had I heard such social passion, such courageous exposure of basic evils, such electric power behind words, such a sweeping challenge to all the values I had been taught to hold highest. From that day forth I was her admirer."[5] These responses, multiplied through the thousands of people that Goldman addressed in her years on the platform and through her published works, confirm her impact in changing the thoughts and feelings of thousands of individuals.

In her own time, she also helped dramatize and publicize vital social issues. Her insistence on her right to speak and her willingness to endure persecution to express that right excited the admiration and assistance of many unimpressed with her anarchism. The result was free speech leagues, which promoted that basic civil right. Her frank public discussion of birth control prompted authorities to arrest her; but Goldman shrewdly used her notoriety and the publicity surrounding the trial to increase popular awareness of that significant issue. Certainly, her repeated lectures on questions related to women and their emancipation heightened public consciousness of feminist issues. Her support for innovations in education and her work in establishing a Ferrer Center in New York stimulated interest in and concern for educational practices. Even her opposition to the conscription law in 1917 provided a useful counterweight to the unbridled patriotism and warmongering of the period. Her true significance often lies not in her ideas themselves but in their contradistinction to the views of her time. Her value was as a stimulus to thought and to discussion on important issues. If Goldman did not persuade Americans to embrace her views, she did challenge their complacency and self-confidence. Bringing issues and attitudes to the fore which unsettled the public, she performed a task crucial to an open society. Often her views were as dogmatic and misguided as those she attacked, but her efforts stimulated creative reaction and response. In essence, Goldman was, as she would have wished, a vital part of the dialectic that produces meaningful, if gradual, social change.

Her work for particular causes often proved vital in assuring their success. For example, her defense of Thomas Mooney, who was accused of bombing a preparedness parade in 1916, probably saved his life. In the same way, her lectures on topics related to workers and their problems reached many persons who were unaware of the difficulties before they heard her. As one woman who heard her speak before a Brooklyn women's group admitted, "She made me feel very strongly the unhappiness about the labor question."[6] Certainly, Goldman was not the only person urging consideration for such causes, but her visibility and her rhetorical skills made her a particularly important ally.

As a dramatic critic, she was successful in making many aware of European playwrights and of significant themes in their works. By encouraging others to read the plays she found so meaningful, Goldman nourished an interest in the arts and in the ideas they explored. As one reviewer noted about her book on the drama, "To the average lay reader, the volume contains swift summaries of certain famous dramas . . . which will do much to incite a reading of the dramas themselves. . . . It is heartily recommended to the students of drama who will be interested in the author's angle of approach."[7] While others were expressing the same notions, Goldman reached a different audience. Those who heard her because of their interest in drama received a healthy dose of anarchism; those who listened because of their anarchist sympathies got a salubrious inoculation of literary culture. That both groups heard her blending of ideology and art was in itself beneficial. Even Will Durant, who confessed that he did not like her personally, found her lectures on drama a valuable antidote to his other pursuits.[8] The drama study groups that developed in the wake of her lectures also encouraged an awareness of and appreciation for worthwhile literary efforts. Van Wyck Brooks's assessment of the impact of her work on drama clearly indicates its significance: "No one did more to spread the new ideas of literary Europe that influenced so many young people in the West as elsewhere."[9] Bernard Smith in his analysis of twentieth-century literary criticism succinctly summarizes her contribution as he notes her limitations:

The essays and lectures on the contemporary theatre . . . were, in fact, very useful in spreading an appreciation of the stage as a social influence and in arousing writers to a realization of their power to move men in the direction of free thought and rational behavior. . . . To Miss Goldman, all of these dramatists were bringing closer the day when there would be no gentility, no superstition, and no exploitation of the poor by the rich. They were the vanguard of a free and intelligent race of men. Miss Goldman was not judging their works for all time, not attempting to discover classic among current productions, and dealing only superficially with esthetic questions. She was intent upon their social significance for the moment, and so it would not bother her that she overrated many of the plays she wrote about—found profundities where there were platitudes, inspiration where there was rhetoric, realism where there was sentimentality. But she did emphatically dig out of them their social value, their moral implications, *for that moment.*[10]

If many of her contemporaries found her frightening and dangerous, others saw her as healthfully provocative. William Marion Reedy, who was editor of the *St. Louis Mirror,* called her "the daughter of the dream" and noted that "she threatens all society that is slavery, all society that is a mask of greed and lust."[11] Floyd Dell outlines her value to her contemporaries even more clearly: "She has a legitimate social function—that of holding before our eyes the ideals of freedom. She is licenced to taunt us with our moral cowardice, to plant in our souls the nettles of remorse at having acquiesced so tamely in the brutal artifice of present-day society."[12] A later assessment of the impact of her work in *Mother*

Eath concludes that the periodical "is a pioneer spokesman for radical thinking in the twentieth century and deserves attention here because of the regard in which both it and its publisher were held by the young radicals of the second decade."[13] Thus, Goldman helped to disseminate radical ideas among the young intellectuals of the day and her status as a speaker as well as her interest in artistic endeavors enhanced her impact.

In essence, for the America of 1900 to 1920, Goldman was a useful stimulus to thought and action. Through her efforts, many people altered their views toward themselves and toward vital social issues. If she gained few converts for anarchism, she did increase public awareness of and sensitivity to pressing social problems. Because of her skill as a speaker, Emma Goldman was able to reach audiences beyond the scope of any single periodical and to carry her radical messages beyond narrow geographic confines. She was, in one sense, the traveling conscience of a nation that often did not appreciate her efforts. Margaret Anderson, who was deeply impressed with Goldman's lectures in Chicago in 1914, offers a fine contemporary assessment of her influence:

And whatever one believes, of one thing I'm certain: whoever means to face the world and its problems intelligently must know something about Emma Goldman. Whether her philosophy will change the face of the earth isn't the supreme issue. As the enemy of all smug contentment, of all blind acquiescence in things as they are, and as the prophet who dares to preach that our failures are not in wrong applications of values but in the values themselves, Emma Goldman is the most challenging spirit in America.[14]

Unfortunately, despite her value as a social critic, Goldman's rhetorical approach probably limited her impact. Her flamboyance and blatant defiance of contemporary codes of behavior repelled some listeners and often attracted audiences who, as she came to realize, wanted to be entertained rather than enlightened. Her strong ideological commitment often led her to be as intolerant and close-minded as those she attacked. Her frequent sarcasm and her clear disdain for her audiences and her readers served to antagonize the very persons she sought to convert. In a very real sense, Goldman's rhetoric interfered with her persuasiveness. Although her techniques served well to stimulate thought and provoke reaction, they were less successful in attracting followers and support. Rhetorically, she was undoubtedly her own worst enemy.

Today, Goldman emerges in a very different light. Because many of her criticisms have been acknowledged as valid and some of the reforms she sought have been instituted, the specific substance of her essays is often dated. But the issues and principles behind her analyses remain timely. As a society, despite some progress, we are still struggling with ways to make our penal systems more humane and effective, for example. The emergence of conservative religious groups as political forces has engendered in many people a fear of the "Puritanism" she attacked so strenuously. The peace movement renews many of the charges and offers many of the same analyses that she provided, although the particular enemies are different. Goldman's writings, thus, retain some value for us, the modern readers, because they address issues that still concern us.

Modern feminists have been quickest to adopt Goldman as their own and to insist on the value of her analyses. In a reminiscence about her contact with Goldman as a young woman, Meridel LeSueur, a journalist and novelist, suggests that Goldman has been "resurrected": "Emma Goldman is one of the strong and strange female figures that have sprung alive in amazing contours in the present woman's movement. I see her now in a new, amazing way, grown alive, a leader of a strange subculture of America, in which images are gestated in one period and emerge in yet another."[15] In essence, the ideals Goldman planted have come to fuller fruition in a new generation, a process that she would see as typical of the enlightenment of anarchism. Although many of her points now seem passé, her focus on the importance of psychological emancipation for women remains enlightening. In the same way, while women now have easy access to birth control techniques and have achieved greater equity in employment, they are faced even more directly with the problem she perceived of how to achieve their full potential as women and as individuals. If Goldman offered no easy answers to these questions, her life and her private struggle to reconcile conflicting forces remain inspiring. Ironically, her autobiography remains interesting not as a history of anarchism (which she envisioned to be its value) but as a chronicle of a personal struggle to live a free life as a woman. As Goldman preached the doctrine of individualism and freedom, she lived it. Her life was true to what she believed. Regardless of our attitude toward her theories, we must respect her personal integrity and her commitment to an ideal. Her life is an inspiration to those who prize such principle and loyalty.

What Goldman provides for modern readers is a clear model of an individual trying to live a life devoted to an ideal. Her searching analysis of problems in the society of her time suggests the value of questioning our own assumptions and practices. Although we may disagree with her views and find her faith in anarchism naive, we can appreciate her decision to commit herself to improving the human condition and to fighting the forces that repressed and limited the individual. Indeed, her argument that humans are caught between two powerful urges—an egocentric goad toward absolute personal freedom and an attraction toward social cooperation—and her insistence that both can be healthful should alert us to our own tendencies to sacrifice one or the other of them.

Finally, Goldman in her ideas, her activities, and her life is a valuable reminder of the importance of diversity and tolerance in a society. Her insistence on the primacy of the individual and on the necessity of personal liberty is at least as valuable in our time as in hers.

In a very real sense, Goldman can continue to serve as our social conscience. Her insights can help us see our own limitations, and her biases and prejudices can remind us of the difficulty of escaping our own preconceptions. In pointing out the error of society's ways and in demonstrating her own, Emma Goldman can be both an inspiration and a warning.

Notes and References

Chapter One

1. *Living My Life* (1931; reprint, New York: Dover, 1970), 10. Further citations from this source are provided in parentheses in the text.
2. Frank Harris, "Emma Goldman, the Famous Anarchist," in *Contemporary Portraits,* 4th ed. (New York: Brentano's, 1923), 225.
3. Emma Goldman to John Haynes Holmes, no date, Emma Goldman Papers, New York Public Library Manuscript Collection, New York. Subsequent references to materials in this collection are indicated as Emma Goldman Papers. The letter is quoted in Alice Wexler, *Emma Goldman: An Intimate Life* (New York: Pantheon Books, 1984), 3. Richard Drinnon, *Rebel in Paradise: A Biography of Emma Goldman* (Chicago: University of Chicago Press), 18–31 also quotes the letter. In addition, Drinnon has a very detailed analysis of Goldman's psychology in "Emma Goldman: A Study in American Radicalism" (Ph.D. diss., University of Minnesota, 1957).
4. Harris, "Emma Goldman, the Famous Anarchist," 226–29. Harris indicates that Goldman listed these episodes in response to his question about "formative influences on her life" prior to the Haymarket executions.
5. Ibid., 229.
6. Wexler, *Emma Goldman: An Intimate Life,* 5–6, 23.
7. Harris, "Emma Goldman, the Famous Anarchist," 230.
8. Goldman spells his name "Kershner" in her autobiography. Drinnon and Wexler use "Kersner," which Wexler indicates is the spelling on his citizenship documents. Wexler, *Emma Goldman: An Intimate Life,* 288.
9. Paul Avrich, *The Haymarket Tragedy* (Princeton: Princeton University Press, 1984), xi.
10. Henry David, *The History of the Haymarket Affair,* 2d ed. (New York: Collier Books, 1958), xix.
11. Ibid., 3–29.
12. Ibid., 7.
13. Ibid., 49.
14. Avrich, *The Haymarket Tragedy,* 39.
15. Ibid.: David also cites the same information in *The History,* 54, 89.
16. Ibid., 64–65.
17. Ibid., 66.
18. Irving L. Horowitz, ed., *The Anarchists* (New York: Dell, 1964), 41. In his introduction, Horowitz comments on Most's pamphlet.
19. Avrich, *The Haymarket Tragedy,* 84, 181–83.

20. Ibid., 190; quote from a revenge circular.

21. Avrich, *The Haymarket Tragedy,* 197–208; David, *The History,* 198–205.

22. David, *The History,* 209, 212, 213; quotes from newspapers.

23. Avrich, *The Haymarket Tragedy,* 215.

24. Ibid., 261.

25. Ibid., 280–82.

26. "Johann Most," *American Mercury,* June 1926, 158.

27. Goldman to Holmes, no date, Emma Goldman Papers.

28. "Johann Most," 158.

29. William O. Reichert, *Partisans of Freedom: A Study in American Anarchism* (Bowling Green, Ohio: Bowling Green University Popular Press, 1976), 371–82. My discussion of Most is based closely on Reichert's. See also, Wexler, *Emma Goldman: An Intimate Life,* 50–52 and Drinnon, *Rebel in Paradise,* 31–35.

30. "Johann Most," 165.

31. Reichert, *Partisans of Freedom,* 407.

32. Wexler, *Emma Goldman: An Intimate Life,* 54–55. My discussion on Berkman's life follows Wexler and Reichert, *Partisans of Freedom,* 407–26.

33. Alexander Berkman, *Prison Memoirs of an Anarchist* (1912; reprint, New York: Schocken Books, 1970), 76.

34. Wexler, *Emma Goldman: An Intimate Life,* 57.

35. Henry David, "Upheaval at Homestead," in *America in Crisis: Fourteen Crucial Episodes in American History,* ed. Daniel Aaron (Hamden, Conn.: Archon Books, 1971), 132–70. My discussion of Homestead is based on David's treatment. Cf. Leon Wolff, *Lockout: The Story of the Homestead Strike of 1892* (New York: Harper & Row, 1965).

36. David, "Upheaval at Homestead," 155.

37. Ibid., 151.

38. Wexler, *Emma Goldman: An Intimate Life,* 84. The quote is from the *Firebrand,* 1 December 1895, an anarchist weekly published in Oregon.

39. Ibid., 86–87.

40. "The Tragedy at Buffalo," *Mother Earth,* October 1906, 15. This essay was originally published in *Free Society,* October 1901.

41. Wexler, *Emma Goldman: An Intimate Life,* 117–18.

42. *Living My Life,* 411. Drinnon, "The Kersner Case," chap. 14 in *Rebel in Paradise* covers this action fully.

43. The affair between Reitman and Goldman was a crucial event in her personal life. For a full treatment of it, see Wexler, *Emma Goldman: An Intimate Life,* 139–61 and Candace Falk, *Love, Anarchy, and Emma Goldman* (New York: Holt, Rinehart & Winston, 1984).

44. *Life,* 16 February 1911 and *Baltimore Sun.* Quoted in flyer for the book. University of California at Los Angeles Collection.

45. Flyer for lecture series. University of California at Los Angeles Collection.

46. "On the Trail," *Mother Earth,* March 1911, 20–21.

47. "Light and Shadows in the Life of an Avante-Guard," *Mother Earth,* March 1910, 20.

48. Harris, "Emma Goldman, the Famous Anarchist," 240–41.

49. "The End of the Odyssey," *Mother Earth,* July 1910, 162–63.

50. "On the Trail," *Mother Earth,* July 1911; "The Power of the Ideal," *Mother Earth,* April 1912, "The Power of the Ideal," *Mother Earth,* July 1912.

51. Wexler, *Emma Goldman: An Intimate Life,* Wexler, 166.

52. Review of "Our New York Activities," *Mother Earth,* April 1914, 54.

53. William M. Reedy, "The Daughter of the Dream," *St. Louis Mirror*; reprinted in *Mother Earth,* December 1908, 355.

54. Cf. Wexler, *Emma Goldman: An Intimate Life,* 209–16 for a fuller discussion of Reitman's activities.

55. Goldman to Inglis, 13 June 1917, Labaidie Collection, University of Michigan, Ann Arbor.

56. Drinnon, *Rebel in Paradise,* 188–89. Goldman's account is in *Living My Life,* 614–21.

57. Wexler, *Emma Goldman: An Intimate Life,* 236; quote from *New York Times,* 11 July 1917.

58. Goldman to Ellen Kennan, 9 April 1922, in *Nowhere at Home. Letters from Exile of Emma Goldman and Alexander Berkman,* ed. Richard and Anna Marie Drinnon (New York: Schocken Books, 1975).

59. Drinnon, *Rebel in Paradise,* 245.

60. Ibid.

61. Ibid., 269–72.

62. Ibid., 275–76.

63. Roger Baldwin to Goldman, 4 December 1933, Emma Goldman Papers.

64. Drinnon, *Rebel in Paradise,* 281–82.

65. Goldman to Alexander Berkman, 27 May 1934, in *Nowhere at Home,* 235.

66. Goldman to Baldwin, 19 June 1935, in *Nowhere at Home,* 59.

67. Goldman to Ben Capes, 21 July 1933, Emma Goldman Papers.

68. Goldman to Berkman, 19 November 1935, in *Nowhere at Home,* 246.

69. Drinnon, *Rebel in Paradise,* 297–300.

70. Ibid., 302–4. See *Vision on Fire: Emma Goldman on the Spanish*

Revolution, ed. with introduction David Potter, (New Paltz, N.Y.: Commonground Press, 1983). This book contains much of Goldman's correspondence *in re* the Spanish Revolution.

71. Drinnon, *Rebel in Paradise,* 313.

72. Harry Weinberger, *Emma Goldman: Speech Delivered at her Funeral, Chicago, May 17th, 1940* Berkeley Heights, N.J.: Oriole Press, 1940. In Labadie Collection, University of Michigan, Ann Arbor.

Chapter Two

1. Hutchins Hapgood, *A Victorian in the Modern World* (1939; reprint, Seattle: University of Washington Press, 1969), 203.

2. Charles A. Madison, *Critics and Crusaders* (New York: Holt, 1947), 226.

3. George Woodcock, "Anarchism: A Historical Introduction," in *The Anarchist Reader,* ed. George Woodcock (Brighton, England: Harvester Press/Humanities Press, 1967); "Anarchism," in *Encyclopedia of Philosophy,* vols. 1–2, ed. Paul Edward (New York: Macmillan, 1967), 113.

4. George Woodcock, *Anarchism: A History of Libertarian Ideas and Movements* (1962; reprint, Cleveland: Meridian Books, 1970), 114–15.

5. Ibid., 113, 120–22, 143–44.

6. Woodcock, "Anarchism: A Historical Introduction," 37.

7. Ibid.

8. Woodcock, "Anarchism," 113.

9. Wexler, *Emma Goldman: An Intimate Life,* 46.

10. Woodcock, *Anarchism: A History,* 95–105.

11. *Living My Life,* 172, 194. Drinnon, "A Study in American Radicalism," 155.

12. Woodcock, "Anarchism: A Historical Introduction," 40–42.

13. Woodcock, *Anarchism: A History,* 184–221.

14. Wexler, *Emma Goldman: An Intimate Life,* 48.

15. *Living My Life,* 74–75.

16. Wexler, *Emma Goldman: An Intimate Life,* 115–16.

17. Ibid., 49.

18. William O. Reichert, *Partisans of Freedom: A Study in American Anarchism* (Bowling Green, Ohio: Bowling Green University Popular Press, 1976), 301–12.

19. *Living My Life,* 173, 219.

20. Wexler, *Emma Goldman: An Intimate Life,* 90. Drinnon in *Rebel in Paradise,* 102 notes that by 1907 Goldman's views had matured.

21. Drinnon, *Rebel in Paradise,* 102; Wexler, *Emma Goldman: An Intimate Life,* 135.

22. Drinnon, *Rebel in Paradise,* 106.

23. Wexler, *Emma Goldman: An Intimate Life*, 137–38; Drinnon, *Rebel in Paradise*, 107–9.

24. Preface in *Anarchism and Other Essays*, (1911; reprint, New York: Dover Books, 1969), 41–42.

25. Ibid., 42–43.

26. "Anarchism: What It Really Stands For," in *Anarchism and Other Essays*, 47. Further citations from this source are provided in parentheses in the text.

27. "Syndicalism: Its Theory and Practice," *Mother Earth*, January 1913, 376; "Syndicalism," *Mother Earth*, February 1913.

28. "The Psychology of Political Violence," in *Anarchism and Other Essays*, 80.

29. Wexler, *Emma Goldman: An Intimate Life*, 91–92.

30. "The Philosophy of Atheism," *Mother Earth*, February 1916, 410.

31. Ibid., 412.

32. "The Failure of Christianity," *Mother Earth*, April 1913, 42.

33. "The Philosophy of Atheism," 415.

34. "Minorities versus Majorities," in *Anarchism and Other Essays*, 69–70. Further citations from this source are provided in parentheses in the text.

35. "The Russian Revolution," *Mother Earth*, April 1917, 41.

36. "The Russian Revolution," *Mother Earth*, December 1917, 2.

37. *The Truth About the Bolysheviki* (Mother Earth Publishing Assoc., 1918), 2.

38. Ibid., 11.

39. "The Crushing of the Russian Revolution," *New York World*, March–April 1922; reprinted as a pamphlet in London in 1922.

40. *My Disillusionment in Russia* (1924; reprint, New York: Thomas Y. Crowell, 1970), 245. Further citations from this source are provided in parentheses in the text.

41. Goldman's involvement in and reaction to the Spanish Revolution in her last years are well documented in a *Vision on Fire: Emma Goldman on the Spanish Revolution*.

42. Ibid., 242.

43. "The Psychology of Political Violence," in *Anarchism and Other Essays*, 107.

44. *My Disillusionment*, xlix.

45. Goldman to Havelock Ellis, 8 November 1925, in *Nowhere at Home*, 69.

46. Goldman to Berkman, 3 July 1928, in *Nowhere at Home*, 90.

47. Goldman to Mark Mratchny, 4 March 1938 and to Comrade Hall, 27 May 1938, in *Nowhere at Home*, 234–35.

48. In her correspondence, Goldman discussed these ideas frequently, and probably resolved them to her satisfaction; but the inconsistency remains in her public utterances.

Chapter Three

1. Wexler, *Emma Goldman: An Intimate Life,* 93–95.
2. Falk's biography of Goldman, *Love, Anarchy, and Emma Goldman* (New York: Holt, Rinehart & Winston, 1984) traces the conflict between her personal and professional life fully. See also Wexler, *Emma Goldman: An Intimate Life,* 139–87.
3. "The Tragedy of Woman's Emancipation," in *Anarchism and Other Essays,* 224.
4. "Marriage and Love," in *Anarchism and Other Essays,* 239. Further citations from this source are provided in parentheses in the text.
5. "Victims of Morality," *Mother Earth,* March 1913, 21.
6. "The Hypocrisy of Puritanism," in *Anarchism and Other Essays,* 171–72.
7. Ibid., 172–73.
8. "The Traffic in Women," in *Anarchism and Other Essays,* 177–78. Further citations from this source are provided in parentheses in the text.
9. "The Tragedy of Woman's Emancipation," 213–14.
10. Ibid., 214–15.
11. Ibid., 217, 219, 221.
12. "Woman Suffrage," in *Anarchism and Other Essays,* 204–5, 208. "The Woman Suffrage Chameleon," *Mother Earth,* May 1917, 78–81.
13. "The Tragedy of Woman's Emancipation," 224–25.
14. *Living My Life,* 553.
15. "The Social Aspects of Birth Control," *Mother Earth,* April 1916, 469, 471.
16. Ibid., 473.
17. Ibid., 472–73.
18. "The Woman Suffrage Chameleon," *Mother Earth,* May 1917, 78–79.
19. Wexler, *Emma Goldman: An Intimate Life,* 196–97; quote from a Goldman letter to her niece, Stella Cominsky.
20. Goldman to Alexander Berkman, in *Nowhere at Home,* 10 September 1925, 134.
21. "The Child and Its Enemies," *Mother Earth,* April 1906, 8.
22. Ibid., 7.
23. Ibid., 10.
24. Ibid., 8–9, 11.

25. "Social Importance of the Modern School," New York Public Library Manuscript Collection; printed in *Red Emma Speaks: Selected Writings and Speeches by Emma Goldman,* ed. Alix Kates Schulman (New York: Times Change Press, 1970), 141.

26. Ibid., 144–46.

27. "La Ruche (The Beehive)," *Mother Earth,* November 1907, 389–90, 390–91, 392.

28. "Francisco Ferrer and the Modern School," in *Anarchism and Other Essays,* 145–66.

29. Goldman's views on political crimes are discussed in chapter 2.

30. "Prisons: A Social Crime and Failure," in *Anarchism and Other Essays,* 111.

31. Ibid., 113–16.

32. Ibid., 111–12.

33. Ibid., 121, 125, 126.

34. "Patriotism: A Menace to Liberty," in *Anarchism and Other Essays,* 127–29, 132.

35. Ibid., 134, 137.

36. Ibid., 137, 138.

37. "Preparedness: The Road to Universal Slaughter," *Mother Earth,* December 1915, 331.

38. "Preparedness: The Road to Universal Slaughter," 331.

39. "Preparedness: The Road to Universal Slaughter," 336, 338.

40. "The Promoters of the War Mania," *Mother Earth,* March 1917, 5.

41. "No Conscription," *Mother Earth,* June 1917, 112.

42. "The Holiday," *Mother Earth,* June 1917, 1.

43. Clipping, no date, Emma Goldman Papers.

Chapter Four

1. Drinnon, *Rebel in Paradise,* 1–10.

2. *Living My Life,* 172.

3. Ibid., 172–73.

4. "The Modern Drama: A Powerful Disseminator of Radical Thought," in *Anarchism and Other Essays,* 271.

5. *The Social Significance of the Modern Drama* (Boston: Richard C. Badger, 1914), 42.

6. "The Modern Drama," 242.

7. "Marriage and Love," 229.

8. "Light and Shadows in the Life of the Avant-Guard," *Mother Earth,* March 1910, 18.

9. *The Social Significance,* 3.

10. Ibid., 80, 273.

11. Ibid., 138, 140, 315, 168.

12. Ibid., 3, 276, 196.

13. *My Disillusionment*, 254.

14. *The Social Significance*, 4–5, 176.

15. Ibid., 4.

16. "The Ups and Downs of an Anarchist Propagandist," *Mother Earth*, August 1913, 173.

17. "The Modern Drama," 241.

18. "The Ups and Downs," 172.

19. *The Social Significance*, 6.

20. *My Disillusionment*, 256–57.

21. *Living My Life*, 377.

22. Georg Brandes, "Henrik Ibsen," *Mother Earth*, September 1906, 39–45; Alvan V. Sanborn, "The Revolutionary Spirit in French Literature," *Mother Earth*, July 1906, 38–56; August 1906, 46–54; September 1906, 46–55.

23. Carl Hamblin, "Edgar Lee Masters," *Mother Earth*, November 1915, 289–90; B. M., "Freidrich Neitzsche," *Mother Earth*, January 1913, 383–89; Charles Mierzwa, "Gustave Flaubert," *Mother Earth*, December 1906, 48–59.

24. *Rebel in Paradise*, Drinnon, 99–101.

25. Wexler, *Emma Goldman: An Intimate Life*, 124.

26. Drinnon, *Rebel in Paradise*, 100.

27. Ibid., 159.

28. "To Our Friends," *Mother Earth*, March 1914, 1.

29. Wexler, *Emma Goldman: An Intimate Life*, 124–25.

30. Drinnon, *Rebel in Paradise*, 101.

31. Frederick J. Hoffman, Charles Allen, and Carolyn F. Ulrich, *The Little Magazine: A History and Bibliography* (Princeton: Princeton University Press, 1946), 148.

32. Walter B. Rideout, *The Radical Novel in the United States* (Cambridge, Mass.: Harvard University Press, 1956), 89.

33. Wexler, *Emma Goldman: An Intimate Life*, 203.

34. "The Modern Drama," 241–42. Further citations from this source are provided in parentheses in the text.

35. *Living My Life*, 527–28. Wexler suggests that Goldman hired the stenographer in *Emma Goldman: An Intimate Life*, 203.

36. *Living My Life*, 528.

37. "The Easiest Way: An Appreciation," *Mother Earth*, May 1909, 86, 88.

38. *The Social Significance*, 69–70. Further citations from this source are provided in parentheses in the text.

39. Cf. Michael Meyer, *Ibsen: A Biography* (New York: Doubleday, 1971), 435–36.

40. Anna W., "Emma Goldman in Washington," *Mother Earth,* May 1916, 517. Cf. Margaret Anderson, "Emma Goldman in Chicago," *Mother Earth,* December 1914, 323.

41. Peter Ure, *Yeats the Playwright* (London: Routledge & Kegan Paul, 1963), 131–32.

42. Meyer, *Ibsen: A Biography,* 435; Leon Schalit, *John Galsworthy: A Survey* (1929; reprint, New York: Haskell House, 1970), 241.

43. Cf. Irina Kirk, *Anton Chekhov* (Boston: Twayne, 1981), 131–53.

44. Alba della Fazia Amoia, *Edmund Rostand* (Boston: G. K. Hall, 1978), 103.

45. *The Social Significance,* 139; Amoia, *Edmund Rostand,* 99.

46. Ernest J. Simmons, *Introduction to Tolstoi's Writings* (Chicago: University of Chicago Press, 1968), 171.

47. Schalit, *John Galsworthy: A Survey,* 233, 238.

48. Ibid., 238.

49. Anderson, "Emma Goldman in Chicago," 320–24.

50. George Middleton, "Snap Shots: Books, Art, Drama," *La Follett's,* 20 June 1914, 7.

51. Bernard Smith, *Forces in American Criticism: A Study in the History of American Literary Thought* (New York: Harcourt Brace, 1939), 293.

52. "Anton Tchekoff," unpublished manuscript, New York Public Library Manuscript Collection.

53. Ashley Dukes, *Modern Dramatists* (1912; reprint, Freeport, N.Y.: Books for Libraries, 1967). Cf. Ludwig Lewisohn, *The Modern Drama* (New York: B. W. Huebsch, 1915); and Archibald Henderson, *European Dramatists* (New York: Appleton, 1926).

Chapter Five

1. *My Disillusionment in Russia* (1924; reprint, New York: Thomas Y. Crowell Co., 1970), xli. Further citations from this source are provided in parentheses in the text.

2. Angelica Balabanova, *My Life as a Rebel* (New York: Harper and Row, 1938), 254.

3. Drinnon, *Rebel in Paradise,* 244–45; *Living My Life,* 948.

4. H. L. Mencken, "Two Views of Russia," *American Mercury,* May 24 1924, 122–23.

5. *Living My Life,* 964–74. Bertrand Russell's reaction was particularly distressing to Goldman because he had visited her in Russia. *Living My Life,* 794, 970–76.

6. W. A. Swanberg, *Dreiser* (New York: Scribner, 1965), 313. Also see, *Living My Life*, 986.

7. Theodore Dreiser to Van Valkenburgh, 19 June 1927, Emma Goldman Papers.

8. *Living My Life*, v. Further citations from this source are provided in parentheses in the text.

9. Falk, *Love, Anarchy, and Emma Goldman*, 384.

10. Goldman to Stewart Kerr, March 1929, Emma Goldman Papers.

11. Drinnon, *Rebel in Paradise*, 268.

12. Goldman to Mr. White, 10 March 1931, University of California at Los Angeles Collection.

13. Falk, *Love, Anarchy, and Emma Goldman*, 7; quote from a letter of Goldman's to Hapgood.

14. Ibid., 3; quote from a letter of Goldman's to Berkman.

15. Ibid., 380.

16. Ibid., 6–7.

17. Ibid., 385.

18. Waldo Frank, "Elegy for Anarchism," *New Republic*, December 30, 1931, 193.

19. Falk, *Love, Anarchy and Emma Goldman*, 397.

20. Ibid.

21. Patricia Meyers Spacks, "Selves in Hiding," in *Women's Autobiography: Essays in Criticism*, ed. Estelle C. Jelinek (Bloomington: Indiana University Press, 1980), 118.

22. Wexler, *Emma Goldman: An Intimate Life*, xvii.

23. Freda Kirchwey, "Emma Goldman," *Nation* 133 (2 December 1931):612.

24. Charles A. Madison, *Critics and Crusaders* (New York: Fredrick Ungar Publishing Co., 1947), 234.

25. Goldman to John Haynes Holmes, no date, Emma Goldman Papers.

26. Falk, *Love, Anarchy, and Emma Goldman*, 382, 390.

27. Ordway Tead, "Emma Goldman Speaks," *Yale Review*, June 1932, 852.

28. Frank, "Elegy for Anarchism," 193.

29. Goldman to Percival Gerson, 2 July 1932, University of California at Los Angeles Collection.

30. Alfred A. Knopf to Mrs. Crouch, 2 November 1933, Emma Goldman Papers.

31. R. A. Preston, unpublished manuscript, no date, Emma Goldman Papers.

32. R. L. Duffus, "An Anarchist Explains Herself," *New York Times*, 25 October 1931, sec. 4, p. 1.

33. "Old Red," *Time,* 9 November 1931, 69; Frank, "Elegy for Anarchism," 193–94.
34. Madison, *Critics and Crusaders,* 234.
35. Spacks, "Selves in Hiding," 118.
36. Drinnon, *Rebel in Paradise,* 272.

Chapter Six

1. Drinnon, *Rebel in Paradise,* 241; quote from Berkman.
2. *Living My Life,* 6–7.
3. Ibid., 41.
4. Preface to *Anarchism and Other Essays,* 42.
5. Ibid., 43.
6. *The Psychology of Political Violence,* (New York: Mother Earth Publishing Assoc., 1911), 83; "Anarchism: What It Really Stands For," 48; "Woman Suffrage," 208–9.
7. "Marriage and Love," 227.
8. "Prisons: A Social Crime and Failure," 115; "Patriotism: A Menace to Liberty," 142; "The Traffic in Women," 193; "Woman Suffrage," 199.
9. "Patriotism: A Menace to Liberty," 136.
10. Preface in *Anarchism and Other Essays,* 198.
11. "Intellectual Proletarians," *Mother Earth,* February 1914, 366.
12. "Woman Suffrage," 207.
13. "The Failure of Christianity," 44.
14. "The Tragedy of Woman's Emancipation," 223.
15. "Marriage and Love," 236.
16. "The Failure of Christianity," 45–46.
17. "Address to the Jury," in *Red Emma Speaks,* 359–60.
18. "Anarchism: What It Really Stands For," 47.
19. "Minorities versus Majorities," 69.
20. "Marriage and Love," 227.
21. "Woman Suffrage," 193.
22. "Minorities versus Majorities," 69.
23. "Address to the Jury," 361–65.
24. "Victims of Morality," 24.
25. "Francisco Ferrer and the Modern School," 166.
26. "The Failure of Christianity," 42–43.
27. "Patriotism: A Menace to Liberty," 130.
28. "Woman Suffrage," 203.
29. "The Traffic in Women," 182.
30. "Marriage and Love," 235.

31. "Address to the Jury," 367–69.

32. "The Hypocrisy of Puritanism," 169, 174.

33. "Preparedness: The Road to Universal Slaughter," 333.

34. "Francisco Ferrer and the Modern School," 157, 162; "Anarchism," 53.

35. "Address to the Jury," 359–360.

36. Madison, *Critics and Crusaders,* 226.

37. Goldman to John Haynes Holmes, 26 June 1932, Emma Goldman Collection, University of California at Los Angeles.

38. *Baltimore Evening Sun* clipping, no date, Emma Goldman Papers; review of *Anarchism and Other Essays.*

39. "The Failure of Christianity," 41.

40. "Patriotism: A Menace to Liberty," 143; "Anarchism: What It Really Stands For," 57; "The Traffic in Women," 176.

41. "Anarchism: What It Really Stands For," 54; "Minorities versus Majorities," 71.

42. "Was My Life Worth Living," *Harper's,* December 1934; reprinted in *Red Emma Speaks,* 435.

43. "Woman Suffrage," 198.

44. "Minorities versus Majorities," 78.

45. "Notes from the Capitol: Emma Goldman," *Nation,* June 28, 1917, 767.

46. Drinnon, *Rebel in Paradise,* 209.

47. Douglas MacFarlane, " 'Red Emma' Stumps for Anarchy," *Windsor Star* 19 May 1939. The *Windsor Star* was a magazine published in Ontario.

48. "Trials and Speeches of Alexander Berkman and Emma Goldman," 45, Labaidie Collection, University of Michigan, Ann Arbor.

49. "Emma Goldman, 'Home' for Visit After 14 Years' Exile in Europe," *New York Herald Tribune,* 3 February 1934.

50. Roger Baldwin to Elizabeth Berry, quoted in Elizabeth Berry, "Rhetoric for the Cause, The Analysis and Criticism of the Persuasive Discourse of Emma Goldman, Anarchist Agitator 1906–1919," (Ph.D. diss., University of California at Los Angeles, 1969), 133.

51. Margaret Anderson, *My Thirty Years' War,* (1930; reprint, New York: Horizon Press, 1970), 70–71.

52. Hapgood, *A Victorian in the Modern World,* 203.

53. Allen Freeman, "Emma Goldman Talks in A Barn," in *The Suppression of Free Speech in New York and New Jersey,* Labadie Collection, University of Michigan, Ann Arbor.

54. Drinnon, *Rebel in Paradise,* 255.

55. Hapgood, *A Victorian in the Modern World,* 203.

56. Leonard D. Abbott, "The Trial and Conviction of Emma Goldman and Alexander Berkman," *Mother Earth,* July 1917, 134.

57. Drinnon, *Rebel in Paradise,* 215; quote of J. Edgar Hoover.

Chapter Seven

1. *Red Emma Speaks,* 4.

2. Karen Rosenberg, "Emma's Ambiguous Legacy," *Women's Review of Books,* November 1984, 8.

3. Hapgood, *A Victorian in the Modern World,* 203–4.

4. Anderson, *My Thirty Years' War,* 54.

5. Roger Baldwin, "A Challenging Rebel Spirit," *New York Herald Tribune Books,* 25 October 1931 is Baldwin's review of *Living My Life.*

6. "Some Civitas Members Wanted to be 'Thrilled' So Emma Goldman Was Asked to Address Them," *Brooklyn Eagle.* January 1916, Emma Goldman Papers; quote from Mrs. Edward A. Quin.

7. George Middleton, "Snap Shots," *La Follett's,* 20 June 1914, 7.

8. Will Durant, *Transition* (New York: Simon and Schuster, 1927), 152.

9. Van Wyck Brooks, *The Confident Years,* 375.

10. Bernard Smith, *Forces in American Criticism,* 294.

11. Madison, *Critics and Crusaders,* 237; quote from William M. Reedy.

12. Ibid.; quote from Floyd Dell.

13. Hoffman, Allen, and Ulrich, *The Little Magazine,* 337.

14. Anderson, "Challenge of Emma Goldman," 9.

15. Quoted from the introduction to a new edition of *Living My Life* (Salt Lake City: Gibbs M. Smith, 1982), xiii.

Selected Bibliography

PRIMARY SOURCES

1. Published Books and Collections
Anarchism and Other Essays. New York: Mother Earth Publishing Assoc.,
     1911. Reprint. New York: Dover, 1969.
This collection includes:
"Anarchism: What It Really Stands For"
"Minorities versus Majorities"
"The Psychology of Political Violence"
"Prisons: A Social Crime and Failure"
"Patriotism: A Menace to Liberty"
"Francisco Ferrer and the Modern School"
"The Hypocrisy of Puritanism"
"The Traffic in Women"
"Woman Suffrage"
"The Tragedy of Woman's Emancipation"
"Marriage and Love"
"The Modern Drama: A Powerful Disseminator of Radical Thought"
Living My Life. New York: Alfred A. Knopf, 1931. Reprint. New York:
     Dover, 1970.
My Disillusionment in Russia. Garden City, N.Y.: Doubleday, Page, and
     Co., 1923.
My Further Disillusionment in Russia. Garden City, N.Y.: Doubleday, Page,
     and Co., 1924.
Nowhere at Home: Letters from Exile of Emma Goldman and Alexander Berkman.
     Edited by Richard and Anna Marie Drinnon. New York: Schocken
     Books, 1975.
Red Emma Speaks: Selected Writings and Speeches by Emma Goldman. Edited
     by Alix Kates Schulman. New York: Shocken Books, 1983. This
     second edition includes three new essays and an extended editor's
     note about Goldman's feminism.
The Social Significance of the Modern Drama. Boston: Richard C. Badger,
     1914.
The Traffic in Women and Other Essays on Feminism. Edited by Alix Kates
     Schulman. New York: Times Change Press, 1970.
Vision on Fire: Emma Goldman on the Spanish Revolution. Edited by David
     Potter. New Paltz, N.Y.: Commonground Press, 1983.

2. Pamphlets

Unless otherwise indicated, these pamphlets are available in Labadie Collection, University of Michigan.

Anarchism: What It Really Stands For. New York: Mother Earth Publishing Assoc., 1911.

A Beautiful Ideal. Chicago: J. C. Hart Co., 1908.

The Crushing of the Russian Revolution. London: Freedom Press, 1922.

Deportation: Its Meaning and Menace. New York, 1919.

Dos Anos in Russia. New York: Aurora, 1923.

A Fragment of the Prison Experiences of Emma Goldman and Alexander Berkman. New York: Stella Co., 1919.

Marriage and Love. New York: Mother Earth Publishing Assoc., 1914.

Patriotism: A Menace to Liberty. New York: Mother Earth Publishing Assoc., 1908 (?).

Philosophy of Atheism and the Failure of Christianity. New York: Mother Earth Publishing Assoc., 1916.

The Place of the Individual in Society. Chicago: Free Society Forum, 1940.

Preparedness: The Road to Universal Slaughter. New York: Mother Earth Publishing Assoc., 1916.

The Psychology of Political Violence. New York: Mother Earth Publishing Assoc., 1911.

Syndicalism: The Modern Menace to Capitalism. New York: Mother Earth Publishing Assoc., 1913.

La Tragedie de l'emancipation Feminine. Saint Joseph, Orleans, France: La Laborlease, 1914 (?).

Trial and Speeches of Alexander Berkman and Emma Goldman in the United States District Court, in the City of New York, July, 1917. New York: Mother Earth Publishing Assoc., 1917.

Trotsky Protests Too Much. London: Anarchist Communist Federation, 1939 (?).

The Truth about the Bolysheviki. New York: Mother Earth Publishing Assoc., 1918.

Victims of Morality and the Failure of Christianity. New York: Mother Earth Publishing Co., 1913. University of California at Los Angeles Collection.

What I Believe. New York: Mother Earth Publishing Assoc., 1908.

Woman without a Country. Berkeley Heights, N.J.: Oriole Press. Reprint. United Kingdom: Genguegos Press, 1979.

3. Articles in publications other than *Mother Earth*

"Anarchy," *Labor Leader*, 5 June 1897, 19.

"American by Comparison." In *Americans Abroad, 1918–1931*, edited by Peter Neagoe. The Hague: Servire Press, 1932.

"Appeal by Alexander Berkman, Emma Goldman, and Others." In *Letters from Russian Prisons*, edited by Roger Baldwin. New York: Albert and Charles Boni, 1925.

"The Assassination of McKinley." *American Mercury*, September 1931, 53–67.

"Berkman's Last Days." *Vanguard*, August-September 1936, 12–13.

"The Bolshevik Government and the Anarchist." *Freedom*, October 1922.

"Bolsheviks Shooting Anarchists." *Freedom* (London), January 1922.

"Die Masse," *Der Sozialist* (Berlin), 1 August 1911.

"Emma Goldman Defends Her Attack on Henry George." *Road to Freedom*, November 1931.

"Emma Goldman's First Address to the Spanish Comrades at a Mass-Meeting Attended by Ten Thousand People." *CNT-AIT-FAI Boletin de Informacion*, 25 September 1936.

"Enlarged Text of Emma Goldman's Radio Talk in 'Barcelona', 23 September 1936." *CNT-AIT-FAI Boletin de Informacion*, 25 September 1936.

"Johann Most." *American Mercury*, June 1926, 158–66.

"Letters from Prison." In *The Little Review Anthology*, edited by Margaret Anderson. New York: Hermitage Press, 1953.

"Madrid Is the Wonder of the World." *Spain and the World*, 13 October 1937.

"Most Dangerous Woman in the World Views U.S.A. from Europe." *British Guiana New Day Chronicle*, 21 February 1932.

"Naive Anarchist." *New York Times*, 4 July 1937.

"On Spain." *Spanish Revolution*, 21 March 1938.

"Persecution of Russian Anarchists." *Freedom*, August 1922.

Preface. In *Camillo Berneri, Pensieri e battaglie*. Paris: Edito a cura dei Comitato Camillo Berneri, 1938.

"Reflections on the General Strike." *Freedom*, August-September 1926.

"Reports on Spain." *Spanish Revolution*, 6 December 1937.

"Russia." *New York World*, 26 March-4 April 1922.

"Russian Trade Unionism." *Westminster Gazette* (England) 7 April 1925.

"The Soviet Executions." *Vanguard*, October-November 1936, 10.

"The Soviet Political Machine." *Spain and the World*, 4 June 1937, 3.

"There Is No Communism in Russia." *American Mercury*, April 1935, 393–401.

"The Tragedy of the Political Exiles." *Nation*, 10 October 1934, 401–2.

"The Voyage of the Buford." *American Mercury*, July 1931, 276–86.

"Was My Life Worth Living?" *Harper's*, December 1934, 52–58.

"What I Believe." *New York World*, 19 July 1908.

"Whom the Gods Wish to Destroy The First Strike Mad." *CNT-AIT-FAI Boletin de Informacion*, 6 October 1936.

"Women of the Russian Revolution." *Time and Tide* (England), 8 May 1924, 452.

4. Major Articles in *Mother Earth* (chronological order)
"The Tragedy of Woman's Emancipation." 1 (March 1906):9–18.
"The Child and Its Enemies." 1 (April 1906):7–14.
"La Ruche (The Beehive)." 2 (November 1907):388–94.
"The Easiest Way: An Appreciation." 4 (May 1909):86–92.
"Francisco Ferrer." 4 (November 1909):275–77.
"The White Slave Traffic." 4 (January 1910):344–51.
"Syndicalism: Its Theory and Practice." 7 (January 1913):373–78.
"Syndicalism: Its Theory and Practice." 7 (February 1913):417–22.
"Victims of Morality." 8 (March 1913):19–24.
"The Failure of Christianity." 8 (April 1913):41–48.
"Intellectual Proletarians." 8 (February 1914):363–70.
"Preparedness: The Road to Universal Slaughter." 10 (December 1915):331–38.
"The Philosophy of Atheism." 10 (February 1916):410–16.
"The Social Aspects of Birth Control." 11 (April 1916):468–75.
"The Promoters of the War Mania." 12 (March 1917):5–11.
"The Woman Suffrage Chameleon." 12 (May 1917):78–81.
"The Holiday." 12 (June 1917):97.

5. Unpublished Typescripts
Unless otherwise designated, these are in the New York Public Library Manuscript Collection.
"Address to the Delegates at the Extraordinary Congress in Pairs of the I.W.M.A." 13 pps.
"Anton Tchekhoff," 9 pp.
"Buenaventor Durruti: In Memoriam," 5 pp.
"Cause and Possible Cure of Jealousy," 8 pp. Reprinted in *Red Emma Speaks: Selected Writings and Speeches by Emma Goldman.*
"The Credo of Professor Camilo Berneri," 1937 (?).
"Dupes of Politics," 12 pps.
"Heroic Women of the Russian Revolution," 6 pps.
"History of the Drama in America" (Amsterdam: International Institute for Social History).
"Hypocrisy of Charity," 10 pps.
Letter about fundraising for Spain in England. Probably intended for distribution.
"Mistakes of God," 9 pps.
"Social Importance of the Modern School," 9 pps. Reprinted in *Red Emma Speaks: Selected Writings and Speeches by Emma Goldman.*

"Socialism; Caught in the Political Trap," 15 pps. Reprinted in *Red Emma Speaks: Selected Writings and Speeches by Emma Goldman.*
"The Speculators in Starvation," 10 pps.
"Thoreau," fragment.
"The Trotsksy-Fascist 'Putch' in Barcelona," 5 pps; first page missing.
"Vice and the Rosenthal Case," 19 pps.
"Walt Whitman," 10 pps.
"Mary Wollstonecraft: her tragic life and her passionate struggle for freedom," 20 pps.
Untitled essay on children. 9 pps.

SECONDARY SOURCES

1. Biographical and Critical Studies

Berry, Elizabeth. "Rhetoric for the Cause: The Analysis and Criticism of the Persuasive Discourse of Emma Goldman, Anarchist Agitator 1906–1919." Ph.D. diss., University of California at Los Angeles, 1969. A detailed neo-Aristotelian analysis of six samples of Goldman's rhetoric. Concludes that her rhetorical practices related to her anarchist theories, that invention was the most important canon to her, and that logic was her primary means of proof. Indicates her contribution to increasing awareness of issues, particularly of free speech.

Drinnon, Richard. "Emma Goldman: A Study of American Radicalism." Ph.D. diss., University of Minnesota, 1957. Very detailed analysis and critique of the roots and principles of Goldman's anarchism, including her reliance on other theorists. Also, careful yet sympathetic assessment of her radical activities.

————. *Rebel in Paradise: A Biography of Emma Goldman.* Chicago: University of Chicago Press, 1961. Benchmark biography of Goldman. Particularly useful in establishing her activities in the larger political and social context. The "Bibliographic Essay" is extremely useful in pinpointing both materials on Goldman and the issues and events surrounding her activities. An indispensable work for anyone interested in Goldman.

Ewing, Christine Combe. "Emma Goldman's Participation in the Labor Free Speech Fight in San Diego 1912–1915." Master's thesis, University of North Carolina, 1975. Detailed account of Goldman's involvement in this controversy together with a general assessment of her rhetorical practices.

Falk, Candace. *Love, Anarchy, and Emma Goldman.* New York: Holt, Rinehart & Winston, 1984. Traces Goldman's intimate relationships with men, particularly with Ben Reitman, as they are revealed in her recently discovered and unpublished correspondence. While Falk's narrative is helpful in explaining the developments in Goldman's emotional life, her extensive quotations from the letters convey the intensity and tenor of Goldman's attachments.

Ganguli, B. N. *Emma Goldman: A Portrait of a Rebel Woman.* New Delhi: R. N. Sachder at Allied Publisher, 1979. Brief biography of Goldman that focuses on the value and vitality of her anarchist ideas for a modern audience.

Ishill, Joseph. *Emma Goldman: A Challenging Rebel.* Translated by Herman Frank. Berkeley Heights, N.J.: Oriole Press, 1957. A commemorative eulogy by an old friend and labor agitator. Focuses on her literary and cultural activities. Originally published in *Freie Arbeiter Stimme,* 1944.

Madison, Charles A. "Emma Goldman: Biographical Sketch." New York: Libertarian Book Club, 1960. Reprint from *Critics and Crusaders.* New York: Fredrick Ungar Publishing Co., 1947. Sympathetic report of Goldman's activism, which commends her idealism, integrity, and concern for social issues.

McManus, Mark. "The Rhetorical Failure of Emma Goldman: A Dramatistic and Dialectic Conflict Analysis." Master's thesis, Auburn University, 1982. Explores Goldman's role as the rhetorical leader of the anarchist movement and argues that she failed to adapt her persuasive strategies to different phases of the movement's development.

Rosenberg, Karen. "The 'autumnal love' of Red Emma." *Harvard* January-February, 1984, 52–56. Based on unpublished letters in Radcliffe's Schlesinger Library. Traces Goldman's relationship with Leo Malmed, whom she identified as Leon Bass in her autobiography, from 1906 to the late 1920s.

Schulman, Alix Kates. "The Most Dangerous Woman in the World." *Women: A Journal of Liberation* (Spring 1970). Reprinted in *The Traffic in Women and Other Essays on Feminism.* Brief introductory biography that focuses on Goldman's feminism. Useful in connecting her with modern feminist thought and in explaining her basic anarchist theories.

———. *To the Barricades: The Anarchist Life of Emma Goldman.* New York: Thomas Y. Crowell, 1971. A sympathetic biography of Goldman based largely on the autobiography. Provides less material on the historical and social context than Drinnon.

Wexler, Alice. *Emma Goldman: An Intimate Life.* New York: Pantheon Books, 1984. Traces the personal conflicts and intimate aspects of Goldman's life up to her deportation in 1919. Especially helpful in revealing the psychological and emotional sides of Goldman's personality. Wexler's analysis of Goldman's personality is both sympathetic and perceptive. Also contains an extremely detailed list of bibliographic sources, including recently discovered letters of Goldman's. A good counterbalance to Drinnon's more historically and socially detailed biography.

————. "Emma Goldman in Love." *Raritan* (Spring, 1981–82):116–45. Traces Goldman's turbulent relationship with Ben Reitman as it is revealed in their correspondence. All of this material is incorporated into Wexler's biography, but this brief treatment of this particular relationship is quite readable and interesting.

2. Selected Reviews, Essays, and Parts of Books on Goldman

Anderson, Margaret. "The Challenge of Emma Goldman." *Little Review,* May 1914, 5–9. In reporting Goldman's lectures in Chicago, Anderson calls her "the most challenging spirit in America" for her courage and forthright examination of mores and prejudices.

Baldwin, Roger. "A Challenging Rebel Spirit." *New York Herald Tribune,* 25 October 1931. In this review of *Living My Life,* Baldwin calls it "a great woman's story of a brave adventure into successive defeats which read like victories." Remembering her important impact on him as a young man, he extols her dedication and compassion, regretting that "'no place in the world is yet ready for such a spirit.'"

Dell, Floyd. *Women as World Builders.* Reprint. Westport, Conn.: Hyperion Press, 1976. Praises Goldman's radical feminism and activism.

Duffus, R. L. "An Anarchist Herself." *New York Times,* 25 October 1931. In this review of *Living My Life,* although not fully sympathetic to her ideology, Duffus nonetheless appreciates her idealism and deep concern for others, which he feels motivated her activities. Noting the decline of anarchism as a social force, he insists that Goldman was a rare individual, "an original and picturesque personality," and calls her autobiography "one of the great books of its kind."

"Emma Goldman's Faith." *Current Literature,* February 1911, 639. Focusing on her explanation of anarchism and her attitude toward women, this review calls *Anarchism and Other Essays* "a vivid revelation of a unique personality."

Frank, Waldo. "Elegy for Anarchism." *New Republic,* 30 December 1931, 193–94. In his review of *Living My Life,* although praising Goldman's idealism and commitment, Frank criticizes her anarchist beliefs as naive and unrealistic. Despite his negative attitude toward her ideology, he correctly points out her failure in the book to provide clear insights into her own motivations and those of her colleagues.

Freeman, Alden. "Seven Years as a Lecture Manager." Labadie Collection. University of Michigan, Ann Arbor. Recalls his experiences in arranging speakers for various groups and recounts Goldman's "barn speech" when she was denied access to a hall in New York in 1909. Includes a reprint of the newspaper reports of the speech and the controversy over her speaking.

Goldsmith, Margaret. *Seven Women Against the World.* London: Methuen, 1935, 153–82. Brief biography of Goldman that praises her idealism and integrity.

Hapgood, Hutchins. "Emma Goldman's Anarchism." *Bookman,* February 1911, 639. Praising the "poetic truth" contained in *Anarchism and Other Essays,* Hapgood concludes that "every thoughtful person ought to read" this volume because perusal will bring about "greater social sympathy" regardless of one's politics.

Kirchwey, Freda. "Emma Goldman." *Nation,* 2 December 1931, 612–13. This review of Goldman's autobiography traces her power and impact to her intense emotional reactions and energy. Kirchwey praises the book for its frankness and vitality, which make it "a fine piece of writing" and a record of notable personal triumph.

Mannin, Ethel. "Russian Revolutionary Women." In *Women and Revolution.* New York: E. P. Dutton, 1939, 121–31. This general chapter on Russian women as revolutionary leaders praises Goldman's lifelong dedication to social change and gives a brief biography. The entire book is dedicated to Goldman because of her courage, selflessness, and singleness of purpose.

Marsh, Margaret. *Anarchist Women 1870–1920.* Philadelphia: Temple University Press, 1981. Briefly discusses Goldman's work as a propagandist for anarchism, particularly in contrast to the more intellectual Voltairine de Cleyre.

Mencken, H. L. "Two Views of Russia." *American Mercury,* 24 May 1924, 122–23. In this review of *My Disillusionment in Russia,* while commending her writing and idealism, Mencken deplores Goldman's ideological fanaticism that made her, in his assessment, unrealistic and too indignant about her experiences in Russia. Her view is distorted, he feels, by her commitment to "the boozy dream of old Johann Most."

Middleton, George. "Snap Shots: Books, Art, Drama." *La Follette's,* 20 June 1914, 7. Although he acknowledges that Goldman's test of art is its relation to life and admits that her analyses reflect this perspective, Middleton commends *The Social Significance of the Modern Drama* as a "vital, soul-questioning volume which inquires rigorously into our social morality with courage and penetration."

"Old Red." *Time,* 9 November 1931, 69. Offering little real criticism, this unsigned essay suggests that Goldman's autobiography may add "warmth" to the reader's "disapproving admiration" of her.

Reedy, William Marion. "The Daughter of the Dream." *St. Louis Mirror,* 5 November 1908. Reprinted in *Mother Earth,* December 1908, 355–58. Rhapsodic response to Goldman's idealistic vision of anarchism.

Reifert, Gail, and Eugene, M. Dermody. "Emma Goldman." In *Women Who Fought: An American History.* Norwalk, Calif.: Cerritos College, 1978, 171–79. Brief biography of Goldman focusing on her activism.

Spacks, Patricia Meyer. "Selves in Hiding." In *Women's Autobiography.* Edited by Estelle C. Jelinek. Bloomington: Indiana University Press, 1980. Considers Goldman's autobiography along with other roughly contemporary women to explore the tension between public roles and private lives. Contends that Goldman's autobiography is more self-assertive than others.

Speed, J. G. "Anarchists in New York." *Harper's Weekly,* 20 August 1892, 758–67. Reports a brief meeting with Goldman, Peukert, and other anarchists, most of whom Speed concludes are either insane or vicious.

Stillman, Clara Greueing. "Two Worlds." *Hound and Horn,* October-November, 1932, 143–57. In this review of *Living My Life,* although she admits Goldman's courage and idealism, Stillman notes that her historical contributions are limited because of her lack of clear thinking and her overemotionalism. She concludes however that the frankness and vitality of the work make it "perhaps one of the great autobiographies."

"Tattler." "Notes from the Capitol: Emma Goldman." *Nation,* 28 June 1917, 766–67. Comments generally on Goldman's trial and deserved reputation as a troublemaker.

Tead, Ordway. "Red Emma Speaks." *Yale Review,* June 1931, 51–52. Commending *Living My Life* as "compelling and stirring," Tead admits his admiration for Goldman's idealism but criticizes her failure in the book to be adequately "reflective."

"Uncle Sam's Obstreperous Niece." *Literary Digest,* 18 August 1917, 54–57. Caustic comment on Goldman's release on bail after her 1917 trial. Pictures her as unprincipled and dangerous.

Weinberger, Harry. *Emma Goldman: Speech Delivered at Her Funeral, Chicago, May 17, 1940.* Berkeley Heights, New Jersey: Oriole Press, 1940. In Labadie Collection, University of Michigan, Ann Arbor. Eulogy by her long-time friend and lawyer. Extols her dedication to principle and her courage.

Wellington, Grace Kemmerling. "Book Review." *Road to Freedom,* February 1932, 7. In an extremely enthusiastic and completely uncritical review, the author labels Goldman's autobiography "a magnificent production, of monumental importance . . . a major contribution . . . to the Anarchist movement and to the world of letters."

Index